Any Means Necessary

Kefi Chadwick is a multi-award-winning writer. Her play *Mathematics of the Heart* won Best New Play at Brighton Festival in 2011 and went on to a sell-out run at Theatre 503, London, in 2012. Her two short plays *SexLife* and *La Petite Mort* played at Latitude Festival and in Edinburgh in 2012 and 2013. She created a bespoke piece of theatre for Latitude in 2013 that went on to be developed by the Arts Council and resulted in an interactive show called *How Was It for You?*, which premiered at Brighton Dome in 2015. She has also contributed to Paines Plough's 'Come to Where I'm From' programme. Her first short film, *Cregan*, won at Waterford Film Festival and screened nationally and internationally. Her second, *Girlpower*, won Best Comedy Short at Aesthetica Film Festival 2014 and was also screened nationally and internationally. Her most recent short, *SexLife*, has screened at fifteen Oscar and BAFTA-accredited festivals, including Tribeca in the USA and Encounters in the UK. She is currently developing her first feature film with Ignition Films. She has written for River City for BBC Scotland and is developing further TV projects with Lovely Day, Kudos, Greenacre Films, and Noho Film and TV. She was on the Royal Court Writers' programme and is currently one of the eighteen writers on iWrite, a Creative England initiative that is developing for the screen emerging voices from across the UK.

T0353277

Kefi Chadwick

Any Means Necessary

Bloomsbury Methuen Drama
An imprint of Bloomsbury Publishing Plc

B L O O M S B U R Y

LONDON · OXFORD · NEW YORK · NEW DELHI · SYDNEY

Bloomsbury Methuen Drama

An imprint of Bloomsbury Publishing Plc

50 Bedford Square	1385 Broadway
London	New York
WC1B 3DP	NY 10018
UK	USA

www.bloomsbury.com

BLOOMSBURY **is a registered trademark of Bloomsbury Publishing Plc**

First published 2016

British Library Cataloguing-in-Publication Data

A catalogue record for this book is available from the British Library

ISBN: PB: 978-1-3500-0229-6
ePDF: 978-1-3500-0230-2
ePub: 978-1-3500-0231-9

Library of Congress Cataloging-in-Publication Data

A catalog record for this book is available from the Library of Congress

Typeset by Country Setting, Kingsdown, Kent CT14 8ES

For Alison, Lisa, Helen and Merrick,
and everyone who has been spied upon
by Britain's political secret police

Any Means Necessary, commissioned by Nottingham Playhouse and developed with the support of the Royal Court Theatre, was first performed by Nottingham Playhouse Theatre Company at Nottingham Playhouse on 5 February 2016 with the following cast and creative team:

Mel   Kate Sissons
Dave Cross   Samuel Oatley
Gavin / Jimmy   Nicholas Karimi
Emma / Leanne   Louise-Mai Newberry
Karen   Lily Lowe-Myers
Abby / Cara   Jo Dockery
Bev / Carol   Beatrice Comins

Director   Giles Croft
Designer   Sara Perks
Lighting Designer   Chris Davey
Sound Designer   Adam P. McCready
Video Designer   Andrew Bullett
Dialect Coach   Sally Hague

Any Means Necessary

based on a true story

Characters

Mel Hart, *twenty-three, Sussex*
Dave Cross, *thirty-five, London*
Gavin Long, *forties, Glaswegian*
Karen Mackintosh, *thirty-four, Manchester*
Carol, *Mel's mum, late fifties.*
Abby, *Mel's sister, late twenties*
Jimmy, *early forties, London Cockney*
Cara Duncan, *forties, lawyer for the Met, upper middle class Oxford*
Leanne Burton, *Dave's wife, thirties*
Beverly Thompson, *fifties, London*
Emma Morely, *forties, London*

Ages are the characters' ages on their first appearance in the play.

A number of roles can be doubled, as follows:
Gavin / Jimmy
Emma / Leanne
Bev / Carol
Abby / Cara

Notes

All the worlds contained in the play should co-exist visually in some way throughout the play.

A forward slash (/) indicates that the next character speaks over the rest of the line from that point.

A dash (–) at the end of a line indicates that it is interrupted or broken off.

An ellipsis (. . .) indicates an uncertainty or trailing off.

Scene One

2011.

A hearing in a side room at the Houses of Parliament.

Bev   I met him at a protest meeting in the mid-eighties. I was late that day. The first day I saw him. I wasn't usually late. I loved those meetings. We were all so passionate, so united. I felt I'd found somewhere I belonged. Something I believed in. But that day I felt a bit awkward and he smiled at me. I smiled back because you do, don't you? Someone smiles at you, you smile back. But then he kept looking over at me. Like he couldn't help himself. Gave me this flicker of a wink. That's when I first felt it. (*Beat.*) Waited for me after. Offered me a lift home. That was the thing with the men in them groups, none of them had any money but he had a van so that made him stand out. A gentleman. That's what I thought. That's the word what described him best. He offered me a lift home and that was the beginning. He was so kind. Generous with everything. I didn't have to struggle for his affection. And I wasn't easy to love. I knew that. Proved it over and over. I wanted it so much, I drove people away but I felt like he saw who I really was. If anything, he was drawn to it, wanted to know all about me, inside and out. No one had ever done that before. We used to make plans. You know the kind of thing. Like teenagers. What we'd do when we were old, where we'd live, how many kids we'd have, all that. He felt like the future. And of course there was the protesting. He encouraged me. Drove me on. I felt like that was the part of me he loved best and I wanted him to love me best for always. (*Beat.*) Does that answer the committee's question?

Cara   I have further questions, Beverly.

Scene Two

September 2004.

Gavin *and* **Mel**'s *shared flat.*

Mel   Thought you'd gone.

Gavin   Have you seen my baccy? (*Off* **Mel**'s *look.*) I know, I know . . . I said I'd give up and I am. Just fucking harder than it looks. Wish they'd ban it everywhere. Least then it wouldn't be so easy to get hold of.

Mel   Why don't you just stop?

Gavin   I will. And as soon as I've given up I'm going to start a campaign against British American Tobacco. Bastards!

He rummages on the table. **Mel** *is clock-watching.*

Gavin   What you up to this evening?

Mel   Nothing much.

Gavin   Band on at the Freemasons. The Anti-UVBs. Folk rock against climate change. It's the sound of 2004, apparently.

Mel   I've . . . er . . . I'm waiting for someone.

Gavin *stops looking for his baccy.*

Gavin   Oh aye. Who's that then?

Mel   No one. Really.

Beat. **Gavin**'s *not giving up.*

Mel   Just this guy I met.

Gavin   Oh. Right. Where?

Mel   What?

Gavin   Where d'you meet him?

Mel   On the Kingshore Wood protest last month.

Gavin   Ah yes. The one you told me about.

Mel   That's the one.

Gavin   Thought he lived down south somewhere.

Mel   He does. But he's up here for work so I invited him round.

Gavin   What work's that then?

Mel   Carpentry.

Gavin   Oh aye. And he's come all the way up here to do that?

Mel   Yes.

Gavin *sits down.*

Gavin   I'll wait then. Say hello. Give him a friendly Scottish welcome.

Mel   You don't have to.

Gavin   I know.

Beat.

Mel   He might be ages.

Gavin   I'm sure the Anti-UVBs can start without me.

Beat.

Mel   Gav.

Gavin   What?

Stand-off. She can't quite tell him to go away.

Mel   Fine.

She sits down.

Gavin   Want a beer?

Mel   Go on then.

Gavin *gets two beers out of the fridge.*

Gavin   What's his name again? This carpenter of yours. Not Jesus, is it?

Mel   Dave. Although his last name is Cross, so . . .

Gavin   Very funny. Dave Cross? Not got the same ring as Jesus. What sort of Dave is he then? Lots of Daves in the world. Dangerous Dave. Dodgy Dave. Driver Dave. Dandy Dave. (*Beat.*) I'm out of Ds.

Mel   Just Dave.

Gavin   Right. (*Beat.*) So he's a good carpenter then, Just Dave?

Mel   I wouldn't know.

Gavin   What? He didn't invite you to see his whittlings when you were at Kingshore?

Mel   No, he did not. (*Beat.*) You know you were the one who said . . .

Gavin   Easy. Only joking with you. I'm sure Just Dave's just great. Got to make sure he's on the level though. Can't let some random woo you in the woodland, can I?

A moment of truce.

Mel   He's . . . decent.

Gavin   Decent Dave. There you go. Knew there'd be another D somewhere.

The doorbell rings.

Oh, that's a decent ring, that is. Good firm hand on the bell.

Mel   Be nice.

Gavin   When am I ever anything else?

Mel   All the time.

She pulls a face at him and goes to get the door.

Gavin *gives himself a quick brush down.*

Mel *brings* **Dave** *into the room, talking as she comes.*

Mel   You find us okay?

Dave   Yeah. Number 8 straight from the station, just like you said.

Mel   The walk across the park confuses people sometimes.

Dave   I'm good with parks.

Gavin   There's a claim you don't hear very often. I'm a dab hand with roundabouts myself.

Mel   This is Gavin, my flatmate.

Dave   Ah, the famous Gavin. Alright, mate.

He puts out his hand and **Gavin** *shakes it.*

Gavin   Aye.

Dave   Mel told me all about you.

Mel   Did I?

Dave   Yeah. Gavin, the partner in crime with the whisky, right?

Mel   Can't believe you remembered that.

Dave   Never forget a fellow whisky drinker.

Gavin   Mel says you're called Just Dave.

Mel   Gavin, weren't you going out?

Gavin   I'm sure the majesty of folk rock will wait. Can't start without their audience who I suspect will be just me.

Mel *glares at* **Gavin** *but* **Dave** *just grins.*

Dave   Great. Because I did bring a little something for the weekend that I thought you might like . . .

He pulls a bottle of malt whisky out of his backpack and puts it on the table. **Gavin** *inspects the label and nods in appreciation.*

Gavin   No' bad.

Dave   Bought it when I was working up there a couple of weeks ago. Smooth as you like. Thought of Mel soon as I saw it.

Gavin   Oh aye.

Mel *gets three glasses and puts them on the table.* **Dave** *pours.*

Dave   Fifteen years old. They finish it in Madeira casks. Gives an extra depth to the flavour.

Gavin   Know a bit about whisky, do you?

Dave   Picked up a bit here and there.

Mel *drinks.*

Mel   Oh, that's delicious.

Dave (*reads the label*)   'Drink deep, drink to make your spirit lighter and remember that you drink where angels have been before you; angels and hairy Scotsmen.'

Mel *laughs.*

Gavin   Not all Scotsmen are hairy, you know.

Dave   I'm only reading what it says on the bottle.

Gavin   Don't. If you repeat the stereotype, you're reinforcing it. Words have power.

Dave   Right. Sorry. I just think it tastes good.

Mel   Try it, Gav. You love whisky. (*To* **Dave**.) He joined a whisky club once.

Dave   Did you?

Gavin   Aye. Until I realised it was a load of pretentious bollocks. Only good thing was the free samples. We liked those, didn't we?

Mel   We did.

Dave   This is not pretentious bollocks, I can promise you that.

Gavin   Finish my beer first. Rude to turn one drink over so quickly in favour of another.

He takes a slug of his beer.

So, Mel says you met at Kingshore?

Dave   Yeah.

Gavin   First protest?

Dave   I got involved in some campaigning down in Tower Hamlets but that was my first proper action, yeah.

Gavin   Mel and I, we've done a few protests at Kingshore together. So what's caused your sudden love of trees?

Mel   Gav. Dave doesn't need you interrogating him.

Gavin   I'm not interrogating him. Am I interrogating you?

Dave   Not at all. My dad grew up in Dorset and he used to take us there in the holidays. He was a real doer, my dad. Loved being outside, always cutting back dead wood or fixing fencing or something even in our little garden in Staines. He died . . . suddenly, not that long ago and . . . I wanted to do something for him.

Mel   I'm sorry about your dad.

Dave   'S okay. Happens, doesn't it? Not that you're ever ready. I'd like to think he's got some idea of what I've done in his name.

He pushes the whisky glass towards **Gavin***.*

Dave   Go on. Try it.

A beat while **Gavin** *hesitates. Then he takes the whisky and drinks it.*

Gavin   Aye, no' bad.

Dave   Thought you'd appreciate it.

Mel   That band won't wait for ever, Gavin. Even if you are their only audience member.

Gavin   Alright. I get the message.

He stands up and puts on his jacket.

Gavin   Don't suppose you two want to come with me?

Dave *looks at* **Mel**.

Dave   Whatever Mel wants to do.

Mel   Think we'll stay here.

Gavin   Well, if you change your mind . . . follow the strains of folk rock angst and you'll find me.

He goes. **Mel** *and* **Dave** *are left alone. It's a bit awkward.*

Dave   Seems like a good bloke, Gavin.

Mel   He is.

Dave   Clearly cares about you.

Mel   He can get a bit . . . protective sometimes. He shouldn't . . . he knows he shouldn't. I can take care of myself. But we've looked out for each other for a long time so . . .

Dave   So he's checking me out?

Mel   It's just his way. Anyway, you're my friend. You've every right to be here.

Dave   So I'm your friend?

Mel   Course. You can't spend three days living in a tree house with someone and not call them your friend, can you?

Dave   No. You can't.

A moment between them, then **Dave** *goes over and looks at a photo wall.*

Dave   That you in the black wig?

Mel   Oh God. It was this party we did. Gav's birthday. Gav and I formed this band. I was on drums and he played guitar. Like the White Stripes only . . . you know . . . a bit rubbish. So we called ourselves the Shite Stripes.

They laugh.

Dave   This you in the climbing gear?

Mel   Ages ago.

Dave   Suits you. Standing on a mountain. Like you're in charge of the world. You still climb?

Mel   Not really. I used to but when I moved here . . . I miss it. Beautiful up there. Miles and miles of mountains that no one has ever set foot on. And that quiet. The sound of no sound. Air full of oxygen.

Dave   You could still go. Mountains haven't gone anywhere.

Mel   Gav doesn't climb, thinks it's pointless, and neither does Karen. Not much fun on my own.

Dave   I'll go with you.

Mel   You climb?

Dave   Is that so hard to believe?

Mel   No. I guess not. I didn't have you down as the action man type, that's all.

Dave   Cheeky. I can do all sorts of things. Climb. Sail. Hike.

Mel   Really?

Dave   Yeah. Love all that.

Mel   Me too.

Dave   We could go sometime if you fancy it. You choose a mountain range and I'll drive us. Be a laugh.

Mel   Okay. Yes. I'd love to. You're on. Wow.

Dave   What?

Mel   Just never thought anyone would offer to go climbing with me.

Dave   Full of surprises, me.

Beat.

Mel   You did this last time. We ended up talking all about me and you never got a word in.

Dave   What do you want to know?

Mel   Everything.

Dave   Nothing to tell. Here. As I am today. This is it.

Mel   You must have been somewhere before Kingshore.

Beat.

Dave   I envy you.

Mel   Why?

Dave   Well, you know you've made the right choices. Done the right thing. I'm not like that.

Mel   Then what are you like? (*Beat.*) Sorry. I'm being nosy. It's none of my business. You don't have to tell me anything.

Dave   No no no . . . I want to tell you. I mean, I hardly know you but I trust you and that's mad. When you do . . . what I did, you get used to not trusting or depending on anyone. Always looking over your shoulder. Waiting for something bad to happen or someone to fuck you over. (*Beat.*) I don't want you to look at me differently. Or think less of me.

Mel   I won't judge you. I promise. (*Beat.*) Honestly, you don't have to tell me. Let's talk about something else.

Dave   I was a courier.

Mel   Okay. For what?

Dave   Drugs.

Mel   Oh right. What sort of –

Dave   Cocaine mostly. Used to transport it around Europe. I'm not proud of it but I got into it young and . . . well, you don't think when you're that age, do you? You just see the money. (*Beat.*) I haven't shocked you, have I?

Mel   No. Bit surprised, but . . .

Dave   It's a fucking shit business and . . . I feel dirty for having done it, so what you must think . . .

Mel   You don't do it now, do you?

Dave   No. No. Fuck no. Never again.

Mel   Well, that's what matters, isn't it? You're allowed to make mistakes, you know, as long as you don't keep making them.

Dave   Turned my back on it all a while ago but it's hard to get going again once you've gone off radar. Not got the right references. The right experience. Like starting from scratch. To be honest, I was a bit lost until I went to Kingshore.

Mel   Well, I'm glad you came then. No one cares what you've done before. It's who you are now that matters.

Dave   I hope so.

Mel   I know so.

She pours two shots of the whisky.

To new lives.

Dave   To new lives.

They clink glasses and drink.

Scene Three

November 2004.

The shared flat. **Mel** *is packing up a bag of stuff for an action –
D-locks, keys, stuff like that.* **Gavin** *is smoking.*

Mel   Are you going to help?

Gavin   I am helping.

Mel   Er . . . I think we can safely describe what you're doing
as watching. Helping would require movement of some kind.

Gavin   I'm thinking about how we're going to manage
everything once we're in.

Mel   You should have thought about that before.

Gavin   I did and now I'm thinking about it again.

Mel   You're lazy.

Gavin   That's a judgement on me that you've no right to
make.

Mel   Well, I'm packing everything up and you're sitting on
your arse so . . . I guess I can make that judgement.

Gavin   Is Lover Boy coming?

Mel   He's not my lover.

Gavin   Aye, but he's sniffing around you like a dog on heat.

Mel   Oh my God, you're jealous.

Gavin   What are you talking about? I'm not jealous.

Mel   Yes. You are. It's written all over your face.

Gavin   You're seeing things.

Mel   I'm seeing the green-eyed monster. I know you too
well, Gav.

Gavin   What do you expect? You meet some bloke and next thing you know, he's on this protest and in that action group. I'm surprised he's not scratching at your door every night, like a cat.

Mel   He's a friend. Okay. And he's interested in what we're doing. You're always going on about how more people should give a shit and then when someone comes along who actually does . . . (*Beat.*) I still love you, you know.

Beat.

Gavin   So he really cares about GM, does he?

Mel   Apparently.

Gavin   And if I asked him what exactly genetically modified crops are, he'd know, would he?

Mel   You can ask him. He'll be here in a minute.

Gavin   Thought we were meeting him there.

Mel   He asked to come here and meet up with the others with us.

Gavin   You could have asked me.

Mel   No, actually I couldn't. Because I live here too and if I want someone to meet me here, then I can do that.

Beat while she runs over her list of all the things she needs. **Gavin** *pulls a face at her.*

Mel   I can see you.

She looks up at **Gavin**. *A moment of stand-off. Then she laughs.*

Mel   You're so annoying.

Gavin   Aye, it's my best feature. So what's Lover Boy bringing to the party?

Mel   Stop calling him that.

Gavin   Sorry. Decent Dave.

Mel   He's got a van. He offered to drive us there, and as you never carry anything –

Gavin   Yes, I do –

Mel   I thought it would make it easier.

Gavin   Well, if he's got a van then I guess he's welcome.

A knock at the door. He goes to open it and we hear him burst out laughing.

No no, it's fine really. Come in.

Dave *comes into the room dressed as a giant red herring.*

Mel   Oh my God.

She struggles not to laugh. **Dave** *pulls off the red-herring head and the top bib. Underneath he's wearing a Guns N' Roses band T-shirt.*

Dave   I've fucked it up, haven't I?

Gavin   If that's a Guns N' Roses T-shirt, then yes, you have.

Mel   Why are you wearing that?

Dave   I saw that you'd worn these last time you did an action.

Gavin   No one I know has ever worn a Guns N' Roses T-shirt.

Mel   Gav! (*To* **Dave**.) That was a carbon offsetting action. Because carbon offsetting is a red herring. But GM's totally different.

Gavin   Talking of which, Dave, can I ask you a question about genetic modification?

Mel   No, you can't. You can get him some proper clothes.

Gavin *gives* **Mel** *a sulky look and heads off to get some other clothes for* **Dave**.

Dave   He thinks I'm a total dick, doesn't he?

Mel   Did you bring your van?

Dave   Yeah, it's outside.

Mel   Then he won't think you're a total dick.

Dave *starts to disrobe from his costume.*

Dave   Can't believe I made such a fuck-up.

Mel   Honestly, it's fine. I don't mind people dressing up to make a point but it's not something I do. Why were you looking up old actions?

Dave   Trying to impress you.

Mel   You don't need to impress me.

Dave   But I want to.

Gavin *comes back in with an armful of clothes.*

Gavin   Right, we've got an excellent selection here in a range of colours and styles. Everything is . . .

Sniffs a shirt then throws it over to **Dave**.

Gavin   . . . relatively clean and in reasonably good condition. Take your pick.

He chucks the rest at **Dave**.

Dave   Thanks.

Gavin   Aye, well, don't say I never gave you the shirt off my back.

Mel   We can take everything in Dave's van.

Dave   Got that right, at least.

Mel   Why don't you go and load up, Gav? Do something useful?

Dave *chucks the van keys to* **Gavin** *and he catches them.*

Dave   Good catch.

Gavin   Over-developed hand-to-eye from years of playing pool. Sign of a misspent youth, apparently.

Dave   Love a bit of pool. Give you a game sometime?

Gavin   Well, you can, although Mel here's the one to beat.

Mel   That's true, I am. They call me 'the shark'.

Dave   Then I guess I'll have to play you.

Gavin   She can wear your fish suit. We can paint it like a Great White.

Dave   You're never going to let me live that down, are you?

Gavin   I would but . . . it's too good to let go.

Mel   Gav. The locks.

Gavin   I'm doing it.

He picks up the bag of D-locks and goes.

Dave   Where shall I . . . ?

Mel   Through there.

Dave *goes out to change.* **Karen** *comes in and dumps down a load of heavy bags.*

Karen   Fucking hell! Next time you need extra kit, ask someone a bit closer. Sweating like you wouldn't believe, carrying it up that hill. Why you and Gav can't live at the bottom of the . . . (*Picks up the herring head.*) What the fuck's this?

Mel   Shhh . . . it's Dave's.

Karen   Who's Dave? Oh right. That Dave. Is this his wooing suit?

Mel   What do you mean?

Karen   Well, Gav says he's been following you around like a puppy.

Mel   Gav would say that. He wanted to come on the action today and he's got a van, so . . .

Karen   So it's just about the van then?

Mel   Yes.

Karen   You can't fool me, kid.

She waggles her eyebrows at **Mel**.

Mel   What is it with everyone? He's a friend, that's all. Just a friend.

Karen   You've got loads of friends and they're not all here.

Mel   You are! Anyway, he's new to all this and he's a bit . . . vulnerable. He's had a hard time. His dad died recently and he's not been protesting long and . . . it's good to help people if they want to get involved, isn't it? Welcome them in.

Karen   And you don't fancy him. Not at all?

Beat.

Mel   A bit. I mean he's . . . you know . . . he's nice . . . but I'm not getting in to all that. It's too stressful, and anyway there's enough going on today without getting carried away.

Karen *picks up the fish head.*

Karen   So if it's not part of some weird sex game –

Mel   You're disgusting –

Karen   – why's he brought it?

Mel   He got confused.

Karen   You're not wrong there. What sort of fish is it anyway? Don't look like any fish I know.

Mel   Red herring, I think.

Karen   How did you get herring from that? It's got whiskers. I'd have thought lobster or something. Here. What do you think?

She puts it on, and as she speaks **Dave** *comes back in.*

Karen   Come here my lovely and let me drag you back to my cave for a night of wild –

Mel   Karen.

Karen   – unbridled fishy passion.

Mel   Karen!

Karen   What? Oh. He's not there, is he?

Dave   I am.

Karen   Ah.

Karen *pulls off the head.*

Karen   Sorry. Just messing about, like. Not often you find a giant fish head in your mate's living room. Well, not this one anyway. Vegetarians.

Dave   Yours for a fiver.

Karen   I'm good for cheap fish parts but thanks.

Mel   Karen. This is Dave. Dave, Karen.

Dave   Alright.

He holds out his hand. **Karen** *shakes it.*

Karen   Comrade of the sea. Are those Gav's clothes?

They both look at **Dave**. *The clothes do look odd.*

Dave   Yeah. Why? Do I look like a right twat?

Mel   It's not that bad.

Karen   Long as you're warm, no one'll notice.

Gavin *comes back in and looks at* **Dave**.

Gavin   Tell me I don't look like that in my clothes.

Karen   'Cept for Gav.

Mel   He couldn't look as bad as you do, Gav.

Gavin   If we had time, I'd take offence to that. I pride myself on being king of the well-fitted protest outfit.

Mel   Maybe you can show us later. But now . . . let's go!

They leave.

The sound of people chanting, shouting. Then the sound of a scuffle. Police shouting and protestors shouting back. This merges into a news report.

Newscaster   Protestors scored a significant victory today against GM crops and the huge multinationals behind the controversial technique. After scenes of violence at the site of Cormorant Chemicals near Nottingham, protestors locked themselves into the HQ . . .

But the rest of the coverage is drowned out in whoops and cheers that are coming from . . .

Scene Four

Dave *is sitting on a chair, his leg heavily bandaged.* **Mel** *and* **Gavin** *are sitting around the table.* **Karen** *is also there. They are all a bit muddy and messy but high on adrenalin. Music plays in the background.*

There's a half-empty bottle of whisky on the table. **Dave** *is mid-story.*

Dave   I was running as fast as I could towards the fence when I saw him coming at me out of the corner of my eye so I swerved, right, and I'm really going for it and I thought . . . you know . . . I fucking thought my heart would burst. And I was ahead, right ahead and I could see the fence in front of me . . . and it was like . . . it was like . . . Then this fucking pig appears from nowhere and cuts my legs from under me. One minute I'm running and the next I'm fucking flying . . . I'm not joking, right . . . flying through the air. Then they were all around me, on top of me, batons flying and I'm rolling this way and that and then –

Gavin   – and then I grabbed you and dragged you through the fence.

Dave   Saved my fucking life, mate!

He leans forward and high-fives **Gavin**. *Then* **Gavin** *pulls him in for a hug.*

Gavin   Brothers in arms.

Dave   Brothers in arms.

They hug, then **Gavin** *lets him go and pours more whisky for them all.*

Gavin   To Dave. Who took one for the team.

Dave   To all of you. For getting me back here almost in one piece.

They all do 'Cheers'. **Dave** *settles himself back in his chair and winces in pain.*

Mel   You okay?

Dave   Will be. Don't know how I didn't feel the knee then because it hurts like buggery now.

Karen   Good war wound, that is.

Dave   A smashed-up knee is a small price to pay for victory.

Gavin   'The good shepherd giveth his life for his sheep.'

Karen   Never had you down as religious, Gav.

Gavin   My mother was devout. Drilled it into me when I was a wee 'un. You never forget that stuff once it's in your brain. It's indoctrination.

Mel   No more whisky for you or you'll start quoting Revelations or something.

Gavin   'The great dragon was hurled down – that ancient serpent called the devil, or Satan, who leads the something astray . . . something something hurled to the earth, and his angels with him.' (*Beat.*) Ach. I don't fucking know. If you want more I'll have to Google it.

Mel   Think that's enough.

Gavin   Then let's drink.

He splashes more whisky into glasses and they all do 'Cheers'.

Karen   Give us a song then, Gav.

Mel   Yes!

Gavin   Ach . . .

Karen   Go on. You know I can't resist you when you sing.

Gavin   When you talk to me like that, Karen, I'd do anything.

Gavin *goes off to get his guitar. A silence falls.* **Mel** *looks from* **Karen** *to* **Dave**.

Mel   Today was amazing. (*To* **Dave**.) And you. You were amazing. I thought that copper was going to have a fit when Gav dragged you through the fence, he looked that angry. Best day we've had for ages. You brought us luck, Dave. And you, Karen. I love you guys.

She goes over and hugs them both, **Dave** *last, and she lingers a bit there.*

Karen   You're pissed.

Mel   No, I'm not. Well, yes, I am. But that doesn't mean . . .

Gavin (*offstage*)   Mel! I'm ready.

Mel *turns the music off. The strains of Abba, 'Take a Chance on Me', on guitar.*

Mel   I love it when he does this.

Dave   Abba?

Karen   Oh yes!

Gavin comes back in, wearing a sparkly dress and playing a guitar, with a load of wigs. He throws a wig at each one of them and they put them on. **Dave** *hesitates a minute.*

Gavin   Put it on, pal. No Abba refuseniks in this house. Not even Guns N' Roses fans. In fact especially not a Guns N' Roses fan. Your musical consciousness needs to be raised.

Dave   I'm not really a . . .

Gavin   Put it on!

Dave *puts it on.* **Gavin** *carries on playing Abba's 'Take a Chance on Me'. They all sing along.* **Gavin** *singles* **Dave** *out for the chorus.* **Dave** *sings back at him. They are all helpless with laughter at his take on Abba.*

Gavin *stops playing after the second chorus.*

Karen   Aw. I was just getting started.

Gavin   And far be it from me to stop you but I've got a better idea.

Karen   What's that then?

Gavin   Eighties night at the pub. All the shoulder-pads and backcombing you can handle.

Karen   I'm in.

Gavin *puts the guitar down.*

Gavin   Mel, Dave. You coming?

Mel *looks at* **Dave**.

Mel   We'll be there in a bit.

Gavin   You can't let us dance alone. We started this together, we've got to finish together. That's the whole point.

Mel   And we will. Promise. We'll follow you down.

Gavin   Okay. You better. Or we'll be lonely. (*To* **Karen**.) Come on then, you. Let's get hammered and dance to shit electro pop until our feet bleed.

Gavin *and* **Karen** *leave,* **Gavin** *singing some eighties electro classic.*

Dave   Thanks.

Mel   You didn't look keen.

Dave   It's just the knee. Don't think I'll be dancing for a while. (*Beat.*) Go with them if you want.

Mel   And leave you here on your own after everything that happened today? I'd never do that.

A beat.

Dave   Didn't have Gav down as an Abba fan.

Mel   Oh yes. Huge. Ever since they won Eurovision. Every year we do a big fancy dress party at Christmas and he always goes as Agnetha.

Dave   No way.

Mel   He once wrote to the university to see if he could do a PhD on the importance of Abba's lyrics to British protest but someone had already done it.

Dave   Mental. Bet he makes a great Agnetha.

Mel   Oh, he does. Once seen, never forgotten, that's for sure. Don't laugh. He's very persuasive, Gav. He had you in a Benny and Björn wig before you could say 'Voulez-Vous'.

Dave   He did. (*Beat.*) Fucking loved that, today. Never felt anything like it. The adrenalin and the . . . the . . . fear, but then the excitement too.

Mel   It's an amazing feeling, isn't it. In the build-up, I can feel that buzz starting in my stomach. Like I'm fizzing inside. And once I'm out there it's like nothing else exists but what's happening right now. It's terrifying but it's also . . . incredible.

Dave   Yeah. Like that. Total buzz. Better than alcohol. Better than . . . better than sex!

The word 'sex' causes a brief shift in the atmosphere. Then **Mel** *cuts through it.*

Mel   I was really impressed today. Most people get a bit freaked out when stuff like that happens but you . . . you just dived right in.

Dave   No point being there if you're not going to get stuck in.

Mel   I always think it's like a game. Can we get to the site and D-lock ourselves in before they catch us? It's like tag at school but for real. And once we're locked on, we've won. This one time, Gav and I were doing this airport runway protest. We'd dug ourselves in and we knew they'd get us out in the end but we'd have a few days at least. We sang every song we knew. We could hear all the coppers outside, no idea what to do and there we were, singing. That's when Gav taught me the words to every Abba song ever written. It bonds you, those times. You get to know each other in a way that no one else can ever understand.

Dave   Like me and Gav today.

Mel   Exactly. Like today.

Beat. Her happiness can't help but seep through.

We made the news!

Dave   We did.

Mel   Thousands of people will see that and they'll all be thinking 'What's the fuss about?' and maybe it won't be so easy for some fuck-off corporate to get its way. Makes me so angry when I think about what we're doing to ourselves. People talk about saving the planet. The planet doesn't need saving. The planet's fine. It's been here millions of years before us and it will be here millions of years after. Even in the final throes of the universe, it'll still be there. A huge lump of rock and metal spinning into darkness. It's us that need saving. People. Because we're fragile. We break easily and we're the ones that will be wiped out. We need to be careful or else we'll be gone. (*Beat.*) Sorry, think I am a bit pissed.

Dave   No, you're right. Got to know what you stand for. Otherwise, you just drift along, wondering what the fuck you're doing here.

Mel   Exactly! Be part of something bigger than you . . . something . . . better. (*Beat.*) You know, you say things and it's like my mind is speaking.

Dave   Yeah well. I can't give you some Marxist explanation like Gav but believing in something is what it's all about for me.

Mel   Gav can be far too intellectual for his own good. I love him but he'd sit and argue a point all day long. I prefer it when we get things done. That's when it comes alive.

Dave   Same. (*Beat.*) I found a room. I meant to tell you earlier but what with the fucking fish suit and all . . .

Mel   What? In Nottingham?

Dave   Yeah.

Mel   You're moving here?

Dave   Thought I might make this my base, yeah. If you don't feel that I'm . . . you know . . . I like being around you and Gav and this is where the action is so . . . well, anyway, I didn't say I'd take it . . . just saw it. Thought I'd ask you first, see if it was okay.

Mel   Course it is. I don't own Nottingham and anyway you're more than welcome here as far as I'm concerned.

Dave   What about Gav?

Mel   Oh, you're well in there. He loves a man who can take a baton charge and come up smiling. It's probably his main criterion for a friend.

Dave   I mean, I'm not stepping on his toes. Because I'd hate to think . . .

Mel   No . . . no . . . no toe-stepping is being done. (*Beat.*) So where's the room?

Dave   Just round the corner.

Mel   Right. We'll be seeing a lot of each other then.

Dave   Hopefully.

*He picks up the guitar where **Gavin** has left it and plays a few chords.*

Mel   Can you play?

Dave   A bit.

Mel   Go on then.

Dave   I only really know a couple of songs properly.

Mel   Let's hear it.

Dave *plays part of 'A Wanted Man' by Johnny Cash.*

*As he does so, **Mel** moves closer to him. When she is right in front of him, he stops and puts the guitar down. Then he takes her hand and pulls her towards him and goes to kiss her but she turns away.*

Dave   What's the matter? Have I upset you?

Mel   No. I just don't think this is a good idea.

Dave   Why not?

Mel   We're friends.

Dave   We are.

Mel   I think . . . I think we should leave it at that.

Beat.

Dave   Don't you like me?

Mel   No. I do. It's . . . nothing like that.

Dave   Then what?

Mel   Things like this, they get complicated. I see it happening all around me. Friends hooking up then breaking up and it ruins . . . everything. At the start they like each other and laugh at each other's jokes and dance around to music and then . . . suddenly it's all resentment. I like you too much to want that to happen. So I think . . . I think it's better if we stop here.

Dave   I won't hurt you.

Mel   You can't say that. You don't know.

Dave   Yes. I do. (*Beat.*) I'm scared too.

Mel   Are you?

Dave   I didn't come up here to get involved. Last thing I wanted. But . . . I like you . . . so much. It's worth the risk. Come on. Come here.

Finally **Mel** *lets* **Dave** *pull her into him. He bends his head and kisses her again. She resists for a moment and then gives in and kisses him back. They pull apart.*

Dave   Was that so bad?

Mel   No. It was . . . it was nice.

Dave   Nice? We can do better than that.

He kisses her again, more thoroughly. Then he pulls away.

I watched you today, running wild out there. Never met anyone like you before. You're so . . . beautiful.

Mel   I'm not.

Dave   You are. Like some warrior woman. (*Beat.*) So . . . can I stay?

Mel   Just for tonight?

Dave   Just for tonight.

Scene Five

A week later. November 2004.

A bland hotel room. **Jimmy** *and* **Dave** *sit either side.* **Jimmy** *flicks through the report in front of him.*

Jimmy   A fish suit? A fucking fish suit?

Dave   I got it wrong.

Jimmy We're not paying you to do fancy dress, you know. This isn't fucking *Playdays*. Keep the comedy outfits to a minimum. Fucking embarrassing.

Dave I'm not in serious trouble, am I?

Beat.

Jimmy Everyone makes mistakes. Anyway, I won't be telling anyone and I doubt you will be either so who's to know? But next time, before you do anything like that, check with me. Not sure about something. Ask. Don't know what to do. Call. One fuck-up we can get away with but any more . . .

Dave I'm sorry.

Jimmy Look, I've been where you are. I know what it's like and I understand what this job takes better than any of those pen-pushers back at the station. Just don't do it again, okay?

Dave I won't.

Jimmy Good lad. (*Beat.*) So what was it? A full-on scales job or just a head?

Dave A head and these . . . tights.

Jimmy Tights?

Dave I don't know what I was thinking. I had to borrow clothes and get changed in the kitchen and all sorts.

Jimmy Talk about baptism of fire. (*Beat.*) Like your commitment, though. Take more than an undercover job to get me in a pair of tights I can tell you. So other than that, how was it? Or –

Dave You got my report?

Jimmy I don't mean all that form-filling bollocks. I mean for you, personally. How was it? Because it can be hard, getting the cover straight. Hitting the right tone. Blending in. Stressful. Don't want you to feel overwhelmed by it.

Dave   I wasn't. Once I'd got the clothes sorted . . . it was better than I expected, actually. Shitting myself on the way there but once it all started, it's such a rush you just get stuck in, don't you? It's like you said . . . it's like swimming underwater. When you're under, you don't think about the world up top. Just concentrate on where you're going and try to hold your breath. And when you're back on land, it's like down there doesn't exist.

Jimmy   Knew you'd be good at this. Soon as I saw you. That look in your eye. The glint, the boss calls it. That ability to shape yourself to what's needed. It's a gift. Not everyone can do it. But you . . . you're like me. Born to it. How's the girl?

Dave   Yeah. Good. Think I'm in there.

Jimmy   Remember what I told you. Find what you have in common and build on it. But don't stray too far from who you really are otherwise you'll fuck it up.

Dave   Yeah, yeah, I got that. I like her. We're going climbing next month. She loves it. Haven't been since training but I liked it then, so . . .

Jimmy   Be careful though. Gets tricky if you get too involved.

Dave   Don't worry. I'm well on top of it.

Jimmy   Nice-looking. I'll give you that. Some of that lot, fuck me, I'd need danger money to even look at, let alone . . . But you're alright, yeah? Coping alright?

Dave   Yeah.

Jimmy   And everything at home's okay?

Dave   Yeah, yeah. Sound.

Jimmy   Because you can tell me if you're not. I'm not going to go running behind your back. That's not my job. My job is to take care of you. So you've got to tell me if you're struggling or –

Dave   No, no, I like it, doing something proper. What I always wanted. Been after joining the Unit since I started. I was only eighteen but even then I knew. Worked hard enough to get here. More I can do, the better.

Jimmy   Good man. We really are keeping those fucking bastards from destroying the country. Without us . . . you don't know the half of it yet but you will. (*Beat.*) So you're on the Inverness action with them then?

Dave   Yeah. Doing all the logistics. Picking up the main tents and taking them up there. Rigging the kitchens. Like being on outdoor manoeuvres in training, really.

Jimmy   Be a month out. No days off.

Dave   Not a problem.

Jimmy   Mustard, you are. I was the same. Couldn't do enough. That's what the Unit needs. (*Beat.*) I've got a bit of news in that department. We've been restructured. More . . . autonomous. Still under the public umbrella, financially, but otherwise . . . private company.

Dave   I don't follow.

Jimmy   The Met funds us but other than that we can fuck off. No more Freedom of Information requests, no more public committee oversight bollocks. No having to go cap in hand seeking approval. Means we can get on with the job. No one looking over our shoulder.

Dave   That's a right touch.

Jimmy   Yeah, well. Make full use of it. (*Beat.*) Climbing? While I'm stuck in some grotty hotel room down the road backing you up. Lucky bastard. Best days of my life, being in the field. To be out there, really doing it. Not just sitting on my arse, pushing paper around. (*Beat.*) You've got to get deep under the surface if you're going to do the job properly. Just don't go fucking drowning on me, alright?

He claps **Dave** *on the back and they laugh.*

Scene Six

February 2005.

Mel*'s mum's house.* **Mel** *comes in.*

Mel   Hello? Hello? Mum?

Carol, **Mel***'s mum, comes in and gives* **Mel** *a big hug.*

Carol   You're here already! I thought you'd be hours yet.

Mel   Dave's a very fast driver.

Carol   Where is he?

Mel   Parking the van.

Carol *lets* **Mel** *go and looks at her.*

Carol   You look happy.

Mel   I am.

Carol   Good. No more than you deserve.

Dave *comes in and sticks out his hand.*

Dave   You must be Carol. Nice to meet you.

Carol *shakes his hand.*

Carol   Mel's told me so much about you.

Dave   Has she indeed?

Mel (*bit embarrassed*)   Not really.

Carol   I'm so pleased you could make it to Grandad's eightieth. He's getting a bit old and a bit deaf but he does love to have the whole family around him.

Dave   Thanks for inviting me.

Mel   We got him an audio book of *Lord of the Rings* so he can listen to it when you're out.

Carol   He'll love it. To be honest, he'll just be delighted you're here. He's been driving me mad, asking when you're coming every five minutes. He's even been practising remembering your name, Dave.

Mel   That's an honour. He usually calls me Abby. Is she here yet?

Carol   Arrived an hour ago. She's been chatting to Grandad.

Mel   God, a whole hour of Abby. Poor Grandad. She's probably giving him a makeover.

Carol   If you go in with that attitude . . . (*To* **Dave**.) Abby and Mel don't always see eye to eye.

Mel   Abby works in PR. When we were kids, she used to make up the rules to every game and then change them when she didn't win.

As she says this, **Abby** *comes in. She's the picture of groomed.*

Abby   Mel. You made it. Wasn't sure if you'd get here on time.

Mel   Hi, Abs.

Carol   How's Grandad? Is he ready for his tea?

Abby   He nodded off mid-sentence so I doubt it. It must be brilliant being old. You can be as rude as you like and no one minds. (*Spots* **Dave**.) And who's this?

Mel   This is Dave.

Abby   The elusive boyfriend. At last! Weren't you supposed to come to lunch a couple of months ago?

Dave   Yeah, got caught up. Got to go where the work is. Makes it tricky to plan ahead.

Abby   But you've made it today. I was starting to wonder if you really existed. Do you have a lot of tattoos? Mel loves a tattoo, don't you, Mel?

Mel   Jamie not with you?

Abby   No. We broke up.

Mel   Shame. You seemed so well matched. (*To* **Dave**.)
Jamie came for Mum's birthday last year and spent the entire
afternoon jiggling his balls around.

Abby   He had heat rash.

Mel   Is that what he called it?

Carol   Shall I pour us all some tea? Do you drink tea, Dave?

Dave   I do. Can I help?

Carol   No, no you sit down. I'll do it.

Mel   No milk for me, Mum.

Abby   You're not still vegan, are you? Eating cardboard
and licking pebbles.

Mel   I was never a vegan.

Abby   Vegetarian, whatever. Is this your influence, Dave?

Mel   I can make my own choices. I don't need a man to tell
me what to do.

Abby   What was it that turned you? Tell me. Was it bacon?

She's right but **Mel** *doesn't want to say.*

Carol   Biscuits? Anyone want biscuits?

Abby   I'm fine. No wheat no carbs no sugar for me.

Dave   I'll have a biscuit.

Abby   Did you know that sugar is poison to the body?
I mean it's like a proper drug. Like heroin.

Mel   Like heroin? Really?

Abby   They did this experiment on rats and they literally
ate themselves disabled with sugar. And they put it in all our

food. I mean even bread has sugar in it. How disgusting is that?

Mel   I can't believe you think that sugar is evil and must be destroyed but that power stations and GM crops are okay?

Carol   Melanie . . .

Mel   Seriously. She won't eat carbs because it's bad for her waistline but she happily does PR for a load of consumerist crap that no one wants.

Abby   It's called having a job. / You wouldn't understand.

Dave   These are delicious. / Did you make them yourself?

Abby   We don't all want to live in squalor for ever.

Carol   I did.

Mel   I don't live in squalor.

Dave   I'm impressed.

Abby   That depends on your point of view.

Carol   Mel, did you hear about Abby's promotion? Account director now.

Abby   Senior account director. Not that it matters.

Mel   Great. Do you get your own broomstick?

Abby   Yes. Gold-plated. Comes with a massive bonus.

Carol   Mel, can't you be happy for Abby for once?

Mel   I am. This is me. Being happy for her. This is how it comes.

Abby   She's just jealous.

Mel   Of what?

Abby   Six-figure salary, nice flat, decent haircut –

Mel   There's more to life than money –

Abby   – says everyone who / doesn't earn any.

Dave   I'm rubbish in the kitchen.

Mel   I have every right / to say what I think.

Dave   But I do love a bit of home baking.

Carol   I used to do my own bread / until I got arthritis in my wrist.

Abby   And I have every right not to listen to it. How we shared a room for all those years / and didn't kill each other, I will never understand.

Dave   That must be painful.

Carol   Sorry, Dave. Girls, will you please stop! Dave doesn't need to see you two squabbling away like teenagers.

Abby   Exactly. No one's interested, Mel. Not even Mum.

Carol   That's not true, Abby. I am interested and I support both of you in what you want to do. I'm your mother. That's my job. Why you have to always bring your arguments in here and try and split me in half, I don't understand. Now go and see if Grandad's awake yet and then we can have his cake.

Mel   No, don't send her away thinking she's won. Do you know what, Abby? When all the resources have run out and you can't go . . . go . . . go fucking skiing or straighten your hair or sit in some shitty spa with your shitty mates –

Abby   You don't know anything about my friends –

Mel   – or whatever it is that you do to stop feeling bad about yourself . . . whatever it is . . . when you can't do that . . . you'll wish you'd been on my side.

Abby   I'm going to buy you a razor for Christmas, Mel. Now you've finally got a man the last thing he wants to see is hairy armpits. No matter what he tells you.

Carol   Abby! Grandad!

Abby   I'm going.

She goes.

Carol   Just one time . . . could you and she not . . .

Mel   It's not me. It's her. She brought it up, going on about bloody sugar. She says things deliberately to wind me up.

Carol   Don't rise to it. Don't rise and she'll stop doing it. You know what she's like. She loves a row. If you just let her wash over you –

Mel   Let her think she's won, you mean –

Carol   Then she'll stop. She doesn't really mean it . . .

Mel   Yes, she does . . . (*To* **Dave**.) And you didn't help.

Dave   I've only just met the woman.

Mel   You could have stepped in and supported me. Said that you think I'm right. That what we're doing isn't a pointless waste of time.

Dave   You know I don't think that.

Mel   Abby only cares what men think. She'd have listened to you.

Carol   You do what you believe and she does what she believes. That's all there is to it. She's as strong-willed as you. You'll never change her. You just have to accept her as she is. Now it's Grandad's day. So can we please just try and get along. Okay? (*Beat.*) Okay, Mel?

Mel   Okay.

Carol   Why don't you peel those spuds? Take your anger out on the humble potato.

She goes. **Mel** *slumps down in a chair.*

Mel   Do you know what the worst thing is? Sometimes I think she's right.

Dave   What?

Mel   Sometimes, I look at us all, running around, planning and plotting and talking and I think, 'Does it make any difference?' Why should we spend our lives trying to make the world a better place when that's not what anyone wants?

Dave   They do. They do want it. They just don't want to think about it. They're not brave like you. They can't deal with that stuff every day. It's terrifying. I like to think I'm a big strong bloke but you . . . you do things that scare the shit out of me. (*Beat.*) You're lucky to have this, you know.

Mel   What do you mean?

Dave   To come from somewhere like this. You can say anything you like. Be yourself. Even if it does lead to a row. Wasn't like that for me. In my family there were rules and you had to stick to them or else. No answering back. No disagreeing. Do what you're told and like it. Never occurred to me to question that. Until I met you. (*Beat.*) I got you something. A present. I was going to give it to you when we got back but . . .

He hands her a box. She opens it. It's a butterfly necklace.

Mel   Oh my God. It's beautiful.

Dave   Saw it in this antique shop and thought of you. I asked the guy, the shop owner, where it had come from, just in case . . . you know . . . it had some grisly history or something. He told me he'd got it from this old woman. Apparently, when her husband asked her to marry him, he couldn't afford a ring so he gave her a necklace instead. He'd died a few years before and the woman wanted to pass it on to someone who would keep up the chain and give it to someone they were really in love with. So I told him about you and he let me have it.

Beat.

Mel   What did you say?

Dave   He let me have it?

Mel   Before that.

Dave   Someone they were really in love with?

Mel   Yes, that bit.

Beat.

Dave   Sorry. I know we agreed to keep things casual but . . . when I'm not with you, I think about you all the time like you're the only thought I can have, the only thing I can feel so . . . you know . . . yeah . . . I love you.

Long beat.

Okay, I'm starting to feel like a bit of a cock now.

Mel   I don't want to get confused.

Dave   I'm not trying to confuse you.

Mel   But you do. I can feel myself shaping my thoughts and actions to yours. Like I'm waiting to see your response before I form my own and I don't like that.

Dave   Look, I'm not asking you to say it back. I know you don't feel the same and that's fine. Let's forget this ever happened. Come on, let's go and say happy birthday to your grandad and have a row with Abby about gender politics or something.

Mel   But I do. Feel the same.

Dave   Really?

Beat.

Mel   Yes. I think about you all the time and when I'm with you, I'm happier than when we're apart and sometimes . . . sometimes I watch you cross your legs or turn your head or even smile and . . . I ache inside. If it wasn't so lovely it would be agony.

Dave   Don't look so worried. People search all their lives to feel like this and we've got it right here.

Mel   Yes. Yes, I suppose we do.

They kiss.

Dave   So are you going to actually say it or not?

Mel   I love you.

Dave   What?

Mel   I love you.

Dave   Once more for luck, so you can't change your mind.

Mel   I love you, you idiot.

Scene Seven

March 2005.

Leanne *is absorbed in sorting out laundry when* **Dave** *comes in. He creeps up behind her and then puts his hands over her eyes. She gasps, then recognises him and throws her arms around him.*

Leanne   Oh my God. You said you couldn't make it this month. (*Beat.*) Nothing bad's happened, has it?

Dave   Nothing like that. Got a surprise welfare break.

They kiss.

Leanne   We've missed you. How long have you got?

Dave   Back tomorrow.

Leanne   So you'll see the boys?

Dave   Yeah. But I wanted to see you first.

They kiss more passionately. Then **Leanne** *pulls back and tugs his hair.*

Leanne   I still can't get used to you with that hair!

Dave   I've told you. Got to look the part.

Leanne   I know, but it doesn't mean I have to like it.

Dave   I'll grow it all back when the job's over. Promise.

Leanne   Okay. I'll stop going on about it. So how's it been? Is it getting any easier?

Dave   A bit. Still scared most of the time but . . . what I'm doing it's . . . important so . . . but . . . fuck, it's intense.

Leanne   I wish you could tell me more about it.

Dave   It's not worth it. If anything went wrong, well, the less you know the better.

Leanne   You've still got the photo I gave you?

Dave   Of course. Keep it hidden under my floorboards. When I really miss you I get it out and think about what you're doing – picking the boys up from school or watching telly or whatever – and I try and imagine being here with you. It's the only thing that keeps me going sometimes. So tell me what I've missed this month.

Leanne   Not much really. My life's not exciting like yours.

Dave   It's exciting to me.

Leanne   Ben got an A-star for a history project.

Dave   That's brilliant.

Leanne   He's so smart. We had parents' evening and they were talking about putting him in this special class for gifted children. And Daniel . . . well, you know what he's like. Nothing bothers him. Always sunny and jolly. He's learning this new song at school and last night I went in to his room and he was singing in his sleep.

Dave   I miss seeing them. Knowing what they're doing.

Leanne   You do see them. When you come home.

Dave   I know. But it's not like when you see them every day. You've got to tell me, yes? Anything that happens or stuff they do. Text me or whatever. So I can feel like a bit of me is still here.

Leanne   I will. Of course I will. What time have you got to leave tomorrow?

Dave   Early, probably. Why?

Leanne   Daniel's got show-and-tell at school. He's doing it on you. He's been working on it all week. He's even made some sort of uniform out of his blue pyjamas. Maybe you could take him to school before you go?

Dave *lets her go and moves away.*

Dave   Is he using my name? In the show-and-tell?

Leanne   Not your first name. They'll know your last name because it's the same as his.

Dave   No photos?

Leanne   I'm not stupid.

Dave   Sorry, sorry. I know you're not. I'm just . . . this job makes you paranoid.

Leanne   It's not like they don't know his dad's a police officer.

Dave   I know, but you know what kids are like. What if he says something or tells them something?

Leanne   He doesn't know anything to tell.

Dave   You never know what kids overhear. And he's got sharp eyes, Daniel. He might have seen something or . . . I don't know.

Leanne   He's proud of you. That's why he's doing it.

Dave   I can't take any unnecessary risks. What I'm doing, it's dangerous enough without having to worry about my son's show-and-tell.

Leanne   It's just him in his pyjamas saying you're a hero. How's that dangerous?

Stand-off.

Okay. Okay. I'll tell him not to.

Dave   What if I help him get another show-and-tell together tonight? Will that make up for it?

Leanne   Maybe.

Dave   We'll do it together. It'll be fun. Just me and him. Special project.

Leanne   He'd love that. I think he misses you the most.

Dave   And I miss him. I miss all of you. Come here.

They cuddle.

I came here to surprise you, not upset you.

Leanne   You haven't. It's wonderful to see you.

They kiss.

Dave   What time have you got to pick them up?

Leanne   Three.

Dave   So we've got some time then.

Leanne   We do.

Dave   Then what are we waiting for?

He pushes her gently offstage, **Leanne** *giggling the whole time . . .*

Scene Eight

2011.

Houses of Parliament. **Bev** *stands, facing the audience like they're the committee.*

Cara   Was he your first boyfriend?

Bev   No.

Cara   Your second?

Bev   No. I don't see what that has . . .

Cara   How many men had you had sex with before you met the man in question?

Bev   I don't understand.

Cara   It's not complicated, Beverly. How many men or indeed women had you slept with?

Bev   Never slept with any women. What are you on about?

Cara   Just men then? How many?

Bev   Not many.

Cara   And how many exactly is that?

Bev   I don't know. A few, maybe.

Cara   You must have some idea of how many men you'd had sex with at that point. Or were there too many to remember?

Bev   Nothing like that. Why are you asking me this?

Cara   You claim to be traumatised by the events which would lead one to believe that this relationship was special –

Bev   It was special.

Cara   – and yet you cannot seem to remember how many people you'd had sex with. Nothing very special about that, is there?

Bev   What are you trying to say?

Cara   I'm trying to establish the importance that you attached to your sexual relationships at that time. Not much, it would seem.

Bev   It was over thirty years ago. Who remembers everyone they slept with thirty years ago?

Cara   Are you sure that this man wasn't simply another in a long list of men – most of whom you seem unable to remember – and the idea of him being special is something that you've come up with after the event?

Bev   It weren't like that. I loved him and he told me he loved me and wanted to share a future with me.

Cara   Didn't you just hear what you wanted to hear? He could have been anyone, really, couldn't he?

Bev   That's not true. That's not true.

She breaks down.

Scene Nine

September 2006.

Mel *and* **Karen** *are cooking dinner at the flat.* **Karen** *tastes something.*

Karen   Try this.

Mel *tastes it and winces.*

Mel   More salt, maybe?

Karen   Is it horrible?

Mel   No. It's . . . try adding salt and maybe pepper. Or Tabasco?

Karen   Who the fuck puts Tabasco in veggie bolognese?

Mel   Gav does. He loves it. Puts it on everything. Even cornflakes.

Karen   See, and there I was thinking I knew how disgusting Gav was but that is a whole new level. Well, it's his supper.

She liberally sprinkles in Tabasco.

Mel   I don't dare cook any meat until he's fully moved out.

Karen   Thought he'd already gone.

Mel   He's still got some stuff here and he stops over the odd night. Think he can't quite bear to let go.

Karen Didn't he mind moving out for Dave?

Mel He's not moving out for Dave. He wanted to move further into the countryside and Dave and I . . . well, we thought it would be good if he moved in here. We spend all our time together anyway unless he's working away so it seemed pointless to pay for two places. And I like having him around me. I look at him sitting on the sofa or making a cup of tea and it feels . . . right. Like he's always been here.

Karen *turns and looks at her.*

Karen You're really in love, aren't you?

Mel He's like . . . I hate that expression 'other half' because it implies that we're not fully grown until we're in a couple and I've always believed that people are individuals, not defined by anyone else, but . . . mirror image. That's what I'd say. He's the mirror image of me.

Karen Love a bit of romance, me. Never comes my way, mind.

Mel It will.

Karen Too gobby for most. Don't mind though. I'm shit when I'm in love anyway. Get all moody and that. Although when I look at you and Dave going gooey-eyed over each other . . . I think it might be nice one day.

Mel Sorry. I didn't mean to go on about it.

Karen No, it's good. Seeing it work out. You'll be buying matching slippers and dressing gowns next.

Mel We're not that bad.

Karen You won't be able to help it. One day you'll just look down and there they'll be. Matching outfits.

Mel Okay, that's depressing.

Karen   I'm only kidding. My dark and cynical humour at work. Been spending too much time with Gav. Anyway, you both might look great in grandad tweed.

Mel   I will miss Gav living here.

Karen   You won't miss his smoking. Or his dirty pants on the bathroom floor. Or the way he . . .

Gavin *comes in.*

Gavin   The way I what?

Karen   The way you creep up on people and listen to their conversations. You won't miss that.

Mel   I will. I'll miss everything.

She goes over and hugs him.

Gavin   You're getting soft there, pal.

Mel   Maybe.

Karen   That's love for you. Makes you weak.

Gavin   She's always been in love with me. She should be used to it by now.

Karen   I meant Dave, you dickhead.

Gavin   Oh aye.

He lets go of **Mel**.

Gavin   So, I've been inspecting his woodworking technique for shelves. Can't say I'm that impressed. Bang the fuckers into the wall and hope they stay there seems to be the order of the day.

Mel   I did those ones.

Gavin   He's going to struggle to get all his heavy-rock CDs up there.

Mel   He got rid of those ages ago. It's all Nick Drake and hip-hop now. Same as me. We seem to have two of almost everything!

Gavin   The musical indoctrination is complete. I can die happy.

Dave *comes in.*

Dave   You slagging off my musical taste as usual, Gav?

Gavin   Not at all. I was approving your new direction. Even heard you singing along to 'Voulez-Vous' last time I played it so now I know you're truly one of us. How's my last supper coming along? Better not be wine and wafers else I'll be worried what'll happen to me on the way home.

Karen   It's nearly ready.

Gavin   Then it's time for the speeches.

Dave   Here we go.

Karen   Before we start, I've got some news, actually.

Gavin   Oh aye. What's that then? Not more fucking hearts and flowers. I can't bear it.

Karen   I'm moving.

Mel   Where?

Karen   Down south. London.

Gavin   Doing what?

Karen   Volunteered for Reach. That black kid that was murdered. No one'll listen to the family and that's just wrong. Someone's got to step up and support them and that someone might as well be me.

Dave   That's great.

Gavin   If you feel the call, you've got to go. New starts for us all, looks like.

Mel   It does.

Then **Gavin** *raises his glass.*

Gavin   To Karen off to London, God help her. To me, off to the countryside where I can commune with nature and plot the downfall of capitalist society in peace.

Whoops and cheers.

And to Mel and Dave. Actually, fuck Dave, the fucking shag muppet. To Mel. Love of my life, light of my life, best friend a man could ever have.

They all drink.

Mel   You don't have to go.

Gavin (*to* **Dave**)   You better be fucking good to her. Or I won't think twice about knocking you out, pal. In a pacifist, non-aggressive sort of a way, of course.

Mel   You won't need to do that. We'll be good to each other. (*Beat.*) I still love you, you know.

Gavin   I love you too.

Karen   Now I feel left out.

Mel   And we love you too.

Gavin   I don't. I fucking hate her.

He hugs **Mel** *and* **Karen** *and then opens the circle up to* **Dave**.

Gavin   Come on then, Dave. I know how much you love a wee cuddle.

Dave   Ah, Gav, never knew you cared.

Gavin   I'm only doing this so you don't feel uncomfortable, you do know that?

Dave   Course.

They let go. **Gavin** *raises his glass.*

Gavin   To you and our lovely Mel. Long may you continue.

They all drink.

Dave   To Mel.

Gavin   Oh, you're not going to make a speech, are you?

Dave   Why not? You do. All the time.

Gavin   Ach. Go on then. Democracy in action and all that.

Dave   To Mel. Everything I ever wanted and more. I'm the luckiest man alive.

Mel   Stop it.

Dave   It's true. I am. And thanks to Gav for fucking off to the countryside so I can move in.

Gavin   I'll be back.

Dave   I'm sure you will.

Karen   To Mel and Dave. Before I throw up.

Gavin   To Mel and Dave.

Dave   To Mel and Dave.

Mel   To us.

Mel *and* **Dave** *kiss. Then they all drink.*

Gavin   Right. Let's eat.

As **Mel**, **Karen** *and* **Gavin** *sit down,* **Leanne** *appears in her space. And takes out her phone and checks it.*

Dave *is caught out of time. We can see* **Mel**, **Gavin** *and* **Karen** *all talking and laughing but we can't hear them. Music underlines* **Dave***'s moment. He looks at* **Leanne** *but she doesn't see him.*

Leanne *puts her phone away – no messages – and leaves.*

Then **Dave** *turns back to* **Gavin***; their banter can be heard again. Lights down.*

Interval.

Scene Ten

June 2008.

Mel *and* **Dave** *stagger into the housing co-op with backpacks from a trip away. They dump their stuff down.*

Dave   Christ. What did you pack in here? Rocks? (*Beat.*) Seriously?

Mel   Thought I'd bring a bit home as a keepsake. A reminder of where we'd been.

Dave   Come here, you.

Gives her a cuddle.

Nicking rocks off mountains. What are you like?

Mel   I didn't steal them. They were there.

Dave   Tell me next time, so I don't break my back carrying the fuckers.

Mel   I will. (*Looks around the room.*) Funny, being abroad. Whilst we were there, I forgot all about England but now we're back . . . feels like being there was just a dream.

Dave   You okay?

Mel   Yes. Yes. Just . . . this place looks so small now. And it smells funny.

Dave   Does it?

Mel   It doesn't smell like home. It smells . . . different.

Dave   It doesn't smell.

Mel   I didn't say it smells. I said it smells different. Usually it smells a bit of us, burnt toast from breakfast or last night's supper or something, but now . . . it just smells empty.

Dave   That's because it has been empty.

Mel   I know but usually there's some sort of residue, no matter how long we've been away but this time . . . nothing. Like the house has forgotten us.

Dave   It hasn't forgotten us. Tell you what, I'll burn some toast while I make tea. Will that help?

Mel   Yes.

He goes over and hugs her. She sniffs him.

At least you still smell like home.

Dave   Do I?

Mel   Always. Wherever we are. (*Beat.*) I was thinking on the drive back, we could move abroad, you know.

Dave   We could.

Mel   Live on a mountain. Wake up every day and see nothing but blue sky in the morning and hold the stars in the palm of our hands at night.

Dave   Just you and me?

Mel   Just us.

Dave   You'd miss everyone here.

Mel   They could come and visit.

Dave   You'd never get Gav abroad.

Mel   I bet I could. If I really tried. Or we could visit them. Anyway, that's not the point. The point is . . . why don't we do it?

Dave   Move away?

Mel   There's nothing keeping us here. We could live abroad for a year or travel. Do something completely . . . different. Have adventures.

Dave   Dunno. Maybe we should do a few more trips before we make our minds up, eh?

He kisses her.

Mel   But we can think about it?

Dave   No harm in thinking.

Mel   I knew you'd like the idea. (*Beat.*) I should start unpacking. Get a wash on.

Dave   Leave it. I can do it.

Mel   No. It's not fair. You drove.

Dave   I like doing things for you. Sit down. Go on, sit down. I'll make some tea and get the grill on. See if I can get this place to smell of home again.

Mel   Okay.

She sits. He leaves. She gets back up and starts unpacking. She pulls a jacket from the bag and shakes it out. A passport falls from the pocket. She picks it up and looks at it.

Dave *comes back in with tea for her and a beer for him.*

Dave   There isn't any bread. I'll go to the shop. Anything else you want to make it smell more like home? Bacon? Eggs?

Mel   Yeah, fine.

Dave   Mel? (*Beat.*) You okay? What's up?

Mel   Who's David Burton?

Dave   What?

Mel   David Stuart Burton. His passport just fell out of your jacket. (*Leafing through.*) That's your photo. Why have you got this?

Beat.

Dave   It's nothing. Really.

Mel   What do you mean? It's not nothing. Why have you got a passport in a different name?

Dave   I wanted to tell you before but then we were going away and . . .

Mel *looks wary.*

Mel   Tell me what?

Dave   Sit down.

Mel   Why?

Dave   Just . . . please sit down.

Mel *sits down and waits.* **Dave** *paces. He looks shifty.*

Mel   Dave, what's going on?

Dave   I've done a terrible thing.

Beat.

Mel   What? Tell me. There's nothing we can't sort out, I promise.

Dave   I never wanted it to come to this. I really didn't. I never meant to hurt you. You won't like this. You really won't.

Mel   You're scaring me now. Why have you got this? (*Pause.*) Dave, you've got to tell me!

Dave   It's from my old life.

Mel   What do you mean?

Dave   When I used to courier drugs, one of the names I used was David Burton. You can't use your own name. They spot you, see. Check how many times you're in and out of a country and if it's too many . . .

Mel   But . . . but you said you'd left all that behind?

Dave   And I had. But I met up with this bloke before we went away.

Mel   What bloke?

Dave   Just this bloke I used to know. I bumped into him and he asked if I was still interested in that line of work.

Mel   And what did you say?

Dave   It was a one-off, a lot of money –

Mel   Oh no –

Dave   – so I heard him out. You know how we're always short on funds for actions . . . for living.

Mel   Tell me you said no.

Dave   Of course I did. But when I got back, I went and got the passport out of hiding. I was going to destroy it but . . . then we were going away and I just . . . I forgot. I swear, I swear . . . I never meant to do anything with it. (*Beat.*) You know what you said earlier? That I'm home to you? Well, you're home for me too. Please don't let this have ruined that.

Long pause.

Mel   You can't do that to me. Scare me like that. I didn't know what –

Dave   I know. I know. I'm sorry. I'll never see that guy again. I swear.

Mel   It's not who you are any more.

Dave   I just . . . I lost my footing for a minute.

Mel *gets up and goes and gets a pair of scissors and cuts up the passport.*

Mel   You're a good man. You have to believe that.

Dave   When you say it I do.

Mel   Promise me you won't ever let those thoughts come into your head again. Our life now, this is what matters, this is who you are. You can't look back.

Dave   I won't.

Scene Eleven

July 2008.

The hotel room. **Dave** *comes in. As he does so,* **Jimmy** *starts to sing 'For He's a Jolly Good Fellow'.*

Dave   I don't believe it. Is this why you called me in here?

Jimmy   No flies on you, sunshine.

Dave   Thank fuck for that. Thought I was in for one of your 'special' lectures.

Jimmy   Not today. Today is a celebration.

Hands **Dave** *a beer.*

Jimmy   To you. Longest-serving officer in the Unit.

Dave   I'd have put me suit on if I'd known it was a party.

Jimmy   Fucking suit. You don't own a suit. Cheers.

They drink.

German police pass on their thanks. Closed those fucking Berlin anarchists down right after you left. They'll struggle to organise another demo any time soon.

Dave   Yeah. I saw.

Jimmy   Some of them are looking at time inside. Proper result that. (*Beat.*) What's the matter? You should be over the moon. If they had their way we'd all be living in tepees, drinking our own urine.

Dave   They're hardly fucking criminals, Jim. They want to change the world, not destroy it.

Jimmy   If they're not with us then they're against us and if that's the case then they're fucking extremists and that's worse than criminals. The only militants we want out there are the ones on our side. That's democracy in action. I know it's hard when you've been under a long time but they're not your friends –

Dave   I know. I know. They're my targets.

Jimmy   Never forget it. Even the girl, Mel. Even her.

Dave   No, you're right. You're right.

Jimmy   You're looking tired. Sleeping okay?

Dave   Not really.

Jimmy   I never slept. Not properly. Used to have nightmares something rotten.

Dave   Yeah. Same. Keep having this one dream over and over.

Jimmy   About what?

Dave   Nothing really. Just a dream.

Jimmy   Tell me. I want to know.

Dave   I'm swimming underwater. This place I used to go as a kid. And it's beautiful. The water's that clear, and I'm loving it, really loving it. Then suddenly I can feel my breath running out. So I start to swim up and I can see the light at the surface so I'm kicking and kicking but no matter how hard I try, it feels like it's getting further away. Then suddenly I can't hold my breath any more and I'm drowning and . . . then I wake up. And I'm so frightened I can't even move.

Beat.

Jimmy   Why did you get into this?

Dave   What do you mean?

Jimmy   Well, you had a good job with vice squad. Regular holidays. Decent money. Why did you throw that in for this?

Dave   I wanted to make a difference. Do something important.

Jimmy   And you are. We're special. Got to remember that. Not like those rozzers pounding the beat in their size tens. The boss was in a meeting the other day with the Prime Minister and guess who he asked after?

He looks pointedly at **Dave**.

Dave   No way. Fuck off.

Jimmy   It's true. He's thinking of a special honour for the work you're doing. You want it in writing? I'll get you it in writing.

Dave   An honour? For me?

Jimmy   For the work you've done, yeah. That climate summit and breaking up the GM lot not to mention how you've helped our European friends. You're famous. I'm just the monkey, you're the organ-grinder everyone's talking about. You can have your pick of jobs after this. Might even run the Unit yourself one day.

Dave   No fucking way.

Jimmy   Why not? You know the playbook better than anyone now. Even me.

Dave   You reckon?

Jimmy   You keep going and it's all there for the taking.

Dave   Never thought about what I'd do after. Been so full on.

Jimmy   And you don't have to. You focus on the job in hand and you'll be well looked after, promise you.

Dave   Okay.

Jimmy   Because what we don't want is you cracking up.

Dave   No, I'm not, I'm fine. I'm ready. Whatever needs doing, I'm there.

Jimmy   Good. Because EON Energy has taken us on.

Dave   Oh yeah?

Jimmy   Get this right and we could be looking at bonuses all round. You could take Leanne and the kids to the Caribbean on your next welfare break.

Dave   She'd like that.

Jimmy   You getting on okay? They can get a bit funny, the wives. Bit twitchy.

Dave   She'd like me at home more. But even when I do get there, she doesn't seem happy. Gets angry over the smallest thing. Leaving a plate out or a teabag in the sink. Anything can set her off. And the kids . . . the kids don't know what to make of me.

Jimmy   How long you been married now?

Dave   Thirteen years.

Jimmy   Christ, and she still wants you at home? You've clearly got the magic touch with women, son. Both of mine couldn't wait to see the back me. Look, throw some flowers at it. Or chocolates, if she's that way inclined. Take her out. Treat her. You know what she likes. Use it. Whatever keeps her sweet. Because you'll need your feet on the ground for this one.

Dave   I will. I'll sort it. Thanks. Sorry . . . about what I said before. My head sometimes.

Jimmy   I know that feeling. It gets confusing. But you hang on to me, son. I won't let you go.

Dave   Thanks, Jimmy. Don't know what I'd do without you.

Jimmy   Just doing my job.

Beat.

Dave   The PM was really talking about me?

Jimmy   I'll get it in writing for you for Christmas. You can stick it up on your wall at home. (*Beat.*) Mark my words, make this EON deal right and there'll be more than honours. You'll be a fucking legend.

Scene Twelve

2011.

The Houses of Parliament hearing.

Emma   We met in the early nineties and within a few weeks he'd moved in. It was very intense from the start. He was involved in every aspect of my life. He stands next to me in my mother's wedding photo on her mantelpiece, he teases me in the family videos of my nephew's birthday and he lies about his family to my grandmother in the last video footage I took of her before she died. We met when I volunteered at a centre for social justice, deaths of young black men in custody, police corruption. That sort of thing. He was charming and funny and he pursued me from early on. Everything seemed perfect. We both loved karaoke and card games and camping. He built our kitchen. We went on holidays all over the world.

Cara   Which countries, Emma?

Emma   I'm sorry?

Cara   Which countries did you go to?

Emma   Everywhere. France, Italy, Israel, Thailand, Scotland, Ireland, all over the UK.

Cara   And you had friends in these places?

Emma   Some. Not all.

Cara   What sort of friends?

Emma   What do you mean?

Cara   Were they political in any way?

Emma   They had beliefs, yes.

Cara   Extreme left-wing views?

Emma   I suppose you could say that. Like in all groups, some went further than others.

Cara   Extremists, you could say.

Emma   No, that's not what I said.

Cara   Did you know all the known associates of the people you met?

Emma   I don't follow.

Cara   How likely do you think it was that you knew everyone they were associated with?

Emma   Not very, but they were normal people. Some were political but none were violent.

Cara   But as we have just established, you didn't know what other lives they might have had outside of your friendship?

Emma   No but . . .

Cara   So it is highly likely that they may well have been a threat to this country and to the safety of its population?

Emma   Not highly likely.

Cara   But you've already said that they were political people?

Emma   They were interested in politics, yes.

Cara   Political people are often involved with others who wish to take a more direct route to change. Terrorists, for example?

Emma   They weren't terrorists.

Cara   I think we've established that you cannot say with any certainty who you were mixing with.

Emma   You can't say that. She can't say that.

Scene Thirteen

July 2008.

Mel *is anxiously pacing.* **Dave** *comes in.*

Mel   Where the hell have you been?

Dave   What?

Mel   I've been calling you and calling you. Your phone's been off. I rang round. I rang our friends, asking for you. No one has seen you. You said you'd be back this afternoon.

Dave   I'm sorry. I was in the pub.

Mel   Which pub? Where?

Dave   Does it matter?

Mel   I called everyone. No one had seen you.

Dave   I was with some old mates from London.

Mel   I left messages. Why didn't you call me back?

Dave   My phone died. Can we talk about this tomorrow?

He staggers towards the bedroom.

Mel   Mum's had an accident.

He stops and turns.

Dave   What?

Mel   She fell and hit her head on the fender but it's hard to know . . . it's hard to know what actually . . . what actually . . .

She can't go on. **Dave** *goes over and puts his arms around her and she cries. Then she breaks away.*

Mel   I was going to phone her tomorrow. I thought we could go up there next weekend and I didn't ring her today because . . . Aren't you supposed to have a premonition? Some higher power that tells you to ring or says 'Get in the car and drive,' but even when the phone rang, I didn't think it would be bad news . . .

Dave   She's a tough old bird. She'll pull through.

He cuddles her really tightly.

Mel   Can we go up there now? Can you drive? I know you've been drinking but I don't think I can stay here not knowing . . .

Dave   Of course. We'll go now.

Scene Fourteen

2011.

The Houses of Parliament.

Emma   There's something else I'd like to say.

Beat.

I wanted kids. He said no. The more we talked about it the harder it got. Finally, he agreed to go to counselling. We went for a year. Me begging him to understand why children were so important to me and him resisting every attempt. After he vanished, I went back to see our counsellor to talk to her about him and she showed me what she'd written in her notes when she first met him. It said 'hitman' question mark. I now believe that he was in couple's therapy with his wife at the same time.

Cara   Emma, you've been diagnosed as having acute paranoia.

Emma   What's that got to do with this?

Cara   You are making claims that could well be founded only in your imagination.

Emma   I was diagnosed as a result of what the police did to me.

Cara   But you can't be sure of that. After all, you've only been assessed since the events you claim took place.

Emma   They did take place.

Cara   That's for the hearing to decide.

Emma   They did take place.

Cara   As I said . . . you're here to give evidence but your evidence is a matter of opinion, not fact. Please carry on with your statement.

Emma   After he left, I was devastated. Thought I'd pushed him away by wanting kids. Took me six months to work out who he really was and then I did become paranoid because once I'd opened the door to an impossible truth, everything else became unstable. What was real and what wasn't became impossible to tell. The worst thing was, no one would believe me. Everyone thought I'd had some kind of breakdown and couldn't accept that he just didn't love me, even my family. Have you any idea what that's like to have no one believe you for nearly twenty years and to feel you might be completely mad and yet to somehow know you're sane? That would be enough to make anyone paranoid. (*Beat.*) I was so . . . light when I met him. I had all these ideals and beliefs. That the world should be a fairer place. That I could be part of that. But what happened, it burnt a void inside me. It damaged me and changed me. It made me all the things I never wanted to be.

Scene Fifteen

Early August 2008.

The graveyard near **Carol**'*s house. Just after the funeral.*

Mel *is standing by her mother's grave.* **Dave** *comes over.*

Dave   You ready? I'm going to drive your aunt and Abby back to the house for the tea.

Mel   I can't leave her yet.

Dave   Course not. You stay here. I'll drop them, but then I'll come back for you.

He turns to go.

Mel   What was it like when your dad died?

Dave   Oh, Mel.

Mel   I want to know how I'm supposed to absorb this . . . how I'm supposed to live with this.

Pause.

Dave   It all happened so fast. One minute he was out in the woods, cutting back trees . . . Neighbour found him. Called an ambulance. I was working in London and my phone rang and before it had really sunk in, I was in the car and on the road. No idea what I'd find at the other end. When I got there, he was unconscious. I sat by his bed for hours listening to the machines. The beep of the monitor. The hiss of the ventilator. I was holding his hand and I kept trying to say all the things I never said. Apologise for not being the son he wanted. Not being good enough. But I couldn't find the right words. Then I must have fallen asleep. Something woke me up and I realised he was squeezing my hand. So I called to the nurse. I said, 'He's awake.' But he wasn't. He'd died and as he'd died, his hand had tightened. That's what I'd felt. Some final neurological twitch. I'd nodded off and he'd died.

Mel *goes and hugs him.*

Mel   Sorry, I'm being thoughtless. Didn't mean to drag it all back up for you.

Dave   It's always there in the back of my mind. That's the funny thing. You adjust. Learn to live with it but those feelings of loss never really go away.

Abby *comes in.*

Abby   Melly, I was wondering where you'd gone.

Mel *turns to face her.* **Abby** *goes over and hugs her.*

Mel   I can't believe it.

Abby   Me neither.

Mel   I never realised how much I relied on knowing she was there and now . . .

Abby   I know. (*Beat.*) She was so proud of you.

Mel   And you.

Abby   She was happy if I was happy, but she really lit up when she talked about the things you did. Her daughter, changing the world.

Mel   I must have driven her mad over the years, not doing the normal thing, always promoting a cause or doing an action or signing a petition. Do you remember when I got arrested and I had to call her in the middle of the night for bail? She just got in the car and drove all the way to come and get me. She really believed in me, in what I was doing, what I thought. And I don't know that I ever acknowledged that.

Abby   We were so lucky to have her.

Mel   We were.

Abby   We've still got each other though. We can still be a family. Carry that on, can't we? Stick together more.

Mel   We can.

Abby   I'll come and visit you and I promise to be nice.

Mel   I'll cook you bacon.

Abby   Actually I've gone vegan.

Mel   Really?

Abby   Yes, but I don't need you going on about it, okay?

Mel   I won't.

Abby   Mum would be happy, seeing us like this.

Mel   She would.

Beat.

Dave   Shall I take you back now?

Abby   No, I can drive us. You stay here with Mel. Take good care of her. She's one in a million.

She goes.

Mel   You can never know, can you? When your time will be up. We walk around like we have all the time in the world and all the while it's slipping away from us, days, weeks, years, and we don't see it, we don't see our lives sliding past . . . But now . . . I know that tomorrow I will wake up and my mum won't be here but I will carry on and I don't want to . . . I don't want the clock to keep ticking. I want it to stop, give me time to catch my breath, time to actually feel what this means. I want it to matter. She taught me everything, how to count, how to colour, how to care about people. All this knowledge . . . I've got so much to pass on and no one to pass it on to. I don't want to just disappear and there be nothing left of me. Can you understand that?

Long pause.

Dave   Yes. Yes, I can.

Scene Sixteen

September 2008.

Dave *is on the sofa, playing a computer game.* **Leanne** *comes in and stands next to him. He doesn't notice. She stands in front of him. He 'dies' in the game.*

Dave   Leanne!

Leanne   You haven't been home in nearly three months.

Dave   I've been working.

Leanne   So you say.

Dave   What does that mean?

Leanne   That's all I ever hear from you these days. Text messages that mean nothing. The odd call to the kids and everything always comes back to 'I'm working'.

Dave   You knew when I took the job that it would be like this –

Leanne   Not like this –

Dave   You knew I'd be away –

Leanne   NOT LIKE THIS. Two years, you said. Two years at the most. It's been over four. The kids hardly know who you are. Do you know that? Last time you were home, Ben asked me who that man was in my bed.

Dave   Don't be stupid. He knows who I am.

Leanne   They want to statement Daniel. They're saying he displays unnatural levels of aggression. The other day . . . the other day he stabbed some boy in the arm with a pencil.

Dave   How can I know these things if you don't tell me?

Leanne   I did tell you. When you called at whatever ungodly hour last week, I did tell you but you don't listen to me.

Dave   So? What are they planning to do?

Leanne   He'll have to have special classes and therapeutic sessions and God knows what else. Do you know, when they told me that I felt guilty? Like it was my fault. Like I'd failed him and then I thought 'at least I'm fucking here'!

He goes to put his arms around her. She pushes him away.

Dave   I'm going to make this all come good. I am. I promise.

Leanne   You say that every time. (*Beat.*) Is there someone else?

Dave   What?

Leanne   Because I can feel you slipping away from me in every look and every touch and I feel like I'm going crazy but I just know . . . something is wrong . . . something is so wrong . . .

Dave   It's the job . . . it's just the . . . you don't know what it's like. I feel myself splintering and I don't know how to put myself back together . . . and I'm so frightened that I can't even . . .

He stops. She goes over and puts her arms around him.

Leanne   Hold on to me. You can hold on to me.

Dave   I'm trying to. I'm fucking trying . . .

Beat.

Leanne   Why don't you leave?

Dave   What?

Leanne   Hand in your notice and leave? Get another job.

Dave   Doing what?

Leanne   Something where you come home every night . . . Where you see your kids and your wife and we have dinner together like a normal family.

Dave   Sit behind a desk, pushing paper around? Is that it? DIY at the weekends and Sunday drives and watch the soaps?

Leanne   Yes. Yes. That's exactly what I mean.

Dave   Right from the start, when I joined the force, I wanted this job. You knew that. Took me ten years breaking my balls busting whores and crack houses to get here. Taking shit every day. All I wanted was to excel at something, be remembered for something, but I was nothing. Just a grunt grinding it out day after day. But now . . . Jimmy said that the PM talks about me. Me. Before this I was . . . I was fucking no one. Now people respect me. Every day I'm undercover,

I know I'm doing something important, something that matters –

Leanne   And what about us? What about our lives? Don't we matter?

Dave   Yes, of course you do.

Leanne   Then please, Dave, please please please come home.

Long long pause.

Leanne   You don't want to, do you?

Dave   It's not as simple as that.

Leanne   Yes. Yes it is.

She walks out and he puts his head in his hands.

Scene Seventeen

October 2008.

Jimmy *is waiting. He's clearly been waiting a while.* **Karen** *comes in.*

Jimmy   What time do you call this?

Karen   I got held up.

Beat.

Jimmy   So, where's this month's report on Reach?

Karen   I haven't got it.

Jimmy   You didn't bring it?

Karen   I didn't do it.

Beat.

Jimmy   And are you going to tell me why or am I supposed to guess?

Beat.

Karen   I'm tired, Jimmy.

Jimmy   Tired of what?

Karen   Tired of trying to find a weakness that we can exploit. Of trying to prove that everyone's got something hidden that means they don't matter.

Jimmy   What the fuck are you talking about?

Karen   Have you any idea what it's like for me? Being around a grieving family? Watching them suffer day after day because no one will listen to them or help them understand why their son died?

Jimmy   I can't believe I'm hearing this.

Karen   And I almost can't believe I'm saying it but I can't carry on like this.

Jimmy   What the fuck does that mean? What would you have us do? Let the family accuse us of all sorts and do nothing about it?

Karen   I'm not saying that.

Jimmy   Let them call us all the names under the sun. Slag us off. Cause fucking chaos –

Karen   I'm not saying that!

Jimmy   Then what are you saying? Because I tell you something, all those middle-class bastards up in arms about this, if they'd seen some black kid on the street corner, they'd have crossed the road, held their bag a little tighter, felt their hearts beat a little faster. When he was alive, they'd have been scared of him, it's only now he's dead, anyone gives a shit.

Karen   I give a shit.

Jimmy   About the wrong thing! You want to help minorities? Is that what you want to do?

Karen   The family just wants the truth –

Jimmy   The truth? I'll tell you the truth. You know who's a minority. Us. We're the real fucking minority.

Karen *goes to speak.*

Jimmy   Hear me out! We're discriminated against. Blamed for things that aren't our fault. Spat at. Shouted at. Abused. No one knows what it is to actually do this job apart from us. So we have to stick together. Make sure we look after our own. Close ranks.

Karen   But that's what's wrong. We shouldn't close ranks. When I started in this Unit I thought we were doing the right thing but now . . . we've lost our way. A long time ago and nothing you've said today makes me feel like we can find our way back. Why are we trying to silence every voice of dissent when those voices are asking reasonable questions?

Jimmy   Come on, Karen. I fucking fought for you. Everyone said that women couldn't do this but I defended you, sent you out into the field, backed you all the way. You're a trailblazer. They'll be writing books about you in ten years' time. Look, I'll get you a welfare break, some time off . . .

Karen   No! I don't want time off. I don't want a break. I can't be two people any more. I need to breathe.

Beat.

Jimmy   So what are you saying?

Karen   I want to leave.

Jimmy   What? You think you can just walk away?

Karen   I don't know, but I want to try.

Jimmy   You don't walk out on us. No one walks out on us. You do this and you will regret it. That I can promise you.

Karen   That's a risk I'll have to take.

She goes.

Scene Eighteen

October 2008.

Dave *is pacing in a state of high stress.* **Mel** *comes in, on a massive high, covered in coal dust.*

Dave   Where the hell have you been?

Mel   You'll never guess what we've just done . . .

Dave   I've been calling you. Your phone's been off.

Mel   Just listen.

Dave   You can't vanish on me like that.

Mel *goes over and opens up a laptop.*

Dave   What are you doing?

Mel   Just wait one second.

Dave   I've been worried out of my mind.

Mel   Look.

She goes over to the laptop, finds what she wants online and presses play.

Newscaster   Protestors today brought a power station to a standstill when they occupied a coal train . . .

Dave *looks at her and finally takes in the coal dust on her face and clothes.*

Dave   Was that you?

Mel *nods.*

Mel   Check it out.

Newscaster   And we have with us the Government Energy Minister . . . Minister, given the level of direct resistance to coal power we are now seeing, what are the plans for coal power in this country?

Minister   Coal power is being phased out over the next twenty years in line with international agreement . . .

He's drowned out by **Mel** *whooping with delight. She grabs* **Dave***'s hands.*

Mel   We did that. We've made that happen. Isn't it amazing?

Dave *is utterly silent.* **Mel** *clicks pause on the laptop.*

Mel   Are you okay?

Dave   How the fuck could you do that to me?

Leanne   What?

Dave   You went behind my back. You kept secrets from me. How am I supposed to feel about that?

Mel   Gav and I agreed –

Dave   Oh, so it's all about Gav now, is it?

Mel   – Gav said and I agreed that we should keep it tight. As few people as possible. Every big action in the last four years has failed because the police have been right on top of us. But the small ones get through so we thought we'd do a big action in a small way.

Dave   And you couldn't tell me? Couldn't give me a clue what you were up to? A little heads up. 'Don't worry, Dave, I'll be gone two days but it's all good. I'm just standing in front of a coal train.'

Mel   You don't tell me everything that you do! You disappear all the time and I don't ask. I let you come and go and do what you need to do. Isn't that what this has always been about? Letting each other be ourselves. Allowing us space to do what we want to do without feeling crushed by the other person?

Dave   That doesn't mean you shut me out or hide things from me. I need to know this stuff.

Mel   Why?

Dave   What?

Mel   Why do you need to know everything that I'm doing?

For a minute **Dave** *is nonplussed.*

Dave   I'm scared.

Mel   Of what?

Dave   That you'll leave me.

Mel   I'm not going to leave you. Why would you say that?

Dave   You can't know. You can't know what's around the corner.

Mel   Yes, I can. What's brought this on?

Dave   When I don't know where you are, I think you might never come back.

Mel   I'll always come back. We're going to have a long life together. Do everything we've planned. I'm not going to back out on you. (*Beat.*) I'm sorry. I didn't think you'd be this upset.

Beat.

Dave   Do you know what I think?

Mel   What?

Dave   I think we should do a big action together. Before we do anything else.

Mel   Like what?

Dave   What is the place we always talk about? The place we always see? The biggest thing we could do.

Mel   Ratcliffe?

Dave   Ratcliffe.

Scene Nineteen

October 2008.

Jimmy *and* **Dave** *at a debriefing.*

Jimmy   Ratcliffe! That's spot on, that is. And you'll keep control of this one, yeah.

Dave   I'm doing all the logistics.

Jimmy   Because we are still in the fucking shitter over that coal train.

Dave   I told you I didn't know about the train.

Jimmy   I know that but the boss, he's less sympathetic than me. I've fought your corner and I've got it straight but this . . . this will square it all away. (*Beat.*) Mel won't be there, will she? Because if she is, we'll have to nick her. Don't want you getting upset and losing control.

Dave   She won't be there. I'll make sure of that.

Jimmy   You pull this off and you'll have really earned your stripes with this one.

Dave   You say that every time.

Jimmy   And I mean it every time. We all do. (*Beat.*) Any news from Leanne?

Dave   No.

Jimmy   Seen the kids?

Dave   Couple of times. Feels like someone else's life . . . someone else's family. It's weird. Can't relate to them at all. I know they're mine but . . . they don't like me much either.

Jimmy   You got to try and work that out. You need something to come back to. That's the trouble with being under so long. You lose your bearings. When I come out, I was fucked, don't mind telling you. Utterly fucked. A broken biscuit. Wife had gone and taken the house. I was living in this bedsit near Edgware Road. Proper dump. This one night,

I watched out the window as these two kids beat up this old man. Properly kicked the shit out of him. Before I went in the field I'd have been out there like a shot but . . . that thing, that . . . connection to another human being, I'd lost it. I properly hated myself at that moment. Felt utterly fucking alone. Took me a while to even get out of bed. Then the boss came to see me. Said I could lie there and rot or I could get back to work. So I got back to work. (*Beat.*) Do you know the other thing he said to me then . . . he said an artist is someone who can hold two fundamentally opposing views and still function. I guess that makes us artists. (*Beat.*) I'm proud of you, son. Now get on with Ratcliffe and bring it fucking home!

Jimmy *gives him a pat on the back and* **Dave** *walks off.*

Scene Twenty

Mel *is packing up for the Ratcliffe action and* **Dave** *comes in. During this scene we could see* **Jimmy** *also getting ready for the action – on the phone, pacing, with a big map of the area, ground plans of Ratcliffe etc.*

Dave   Have you got the banner?

Mel *passes a rolled-up banner to him.*

Dave   And the rest of the kit?

Mel *goes off to get it. She comes back in, carrying a heavy bag.*

Dave   Let me get that.

He kisses her.

What's in here?

Mel   Wire-cutters and the rest of the climbing gear. Gav's putting the hammocks in the van. I wish I was coming with you.

Dave   I know, but we need you here to manage the press.

Mel   I know. I know.

Dave *takes the bag from her, looks in it and then ticks off his list.*

Mel   Look at you with your list.

Dave   Can't beat a bit of proper organisation. Chuck those spares in. You never know, we might get longer if we're lucky.

Mel *picks up a bag of something and throws in a plastic bottle.*

Mel   I hate pissing in a bottle.

Dave   Better than pissing on your mate!

They laugh.

Mel   You ready?

Dave   As I'll ever be.

Mel   I can't believe I'm not coming. I'll miss you.

Dave   You'll see me soon enough.

Mel   Hopefully on the news!

Dave *kisses* **Mel** *and then leaves.* **Mel** *waits until he's gone, then she goes.*

The sound of school-hall doors being kicked in, police shouting 'Police – don't move.' The sounds of a scuffle, lots of people shouting, arrest warnings overlapping with chaos. Then the sounds of news reports about the arrests of protestors planning an action at Ratcliffe Power Station.

Scene Twenty-One

April 2009.

A police cell. **Jimmy** *and* **Cara** *are there.* **Dave** *is brought in.*

Dave   What the fuck's going on?

Jimmy   That's not a very nice welcome for the lady.

Dave   You can't bring me in here.

Jimmy   Put your fucking toys back in the pram. You're going back in with the others, pronto. Need to have a chat first.

Dave   Fuck's sake. Now is not the time.

Jimmy *gives him a look.*

Jimmy   Think I'm the best judge of that, don't you? Boss says well done by the way. Top job. All over the press. Action failed. Multiple arrests. It's a fucking disaster for the activists. EON has officially wet their knickers in excitement. You've earned us another ten-year retainer right there.

Dave   Great. Good. Now, can I go back in with the others?

Cara   Not yet, I'm afraid.

Dave   And you are?

Jimmy   This is Cara Duncan, she's going to be acting on your behalf.

Dave   Jesus. Why don't you just buy me a T-shirt that says 'undercover'?

Jimmy   You're overreacting.

Dave   Only five people in that planning group. Just one gets a different lawyer. You don't have to be a detective to work out that something's not right there.

Cara   The Crown Prosecution Service knows what's going on. They'll drop the charges against you.

Dave   Fuck sake. I know what you're saying. How can I carry on if everyone's giving me the squinty eye?

Jimmy   You're not going to. That's the point.

Dave   What?

Jimmy   You're being pulled out.

Dave   No. No. I'm not . . . I can't . . .

Cara   Time to come back to the real world. Don't worry. If anything comes back to you we will resort to our usual position of neither confirming nor denying that you're an undercover officer.

Dave   Can she just fuck off?

Jimmy (*to* **Cara**)   I'll see you downstairs.

Cara   Luckily for you, Dave, I didn't take that personally.

She goes.

Jimmy   I know you're upset but she's on our side, so try not to totally fuck her off before she's done her job, yeah?

Dave   You can't pull me out. What about EON? What about the intel?

Jimmy   We've got someone else ready to come in. Been working their way up in Leeds, going to bring them over here in the next couple of months. (*Off* **Dave**'s *look of surprise.*) You didn't think you were the only one? You and me, we're just cogs in the machine and the machine goes on long after we're gone.

Dave   But I can't just –

Jimmy   Yes. You can. You get out of here and you start your exit strategy and in three weeks, you're gone. Understand? (*Beat.*) Right, we'll put you back with the others now.

Dave   Once I come out, what happens to me?

Jimmy   What do you mean?

Dave   I mean what happens to me? What do I do?

Jimmy   How the fuck would I know? That's for personnel to decide.

Dave   What?

Jimmy   I'll write you a good reference. They might be able to sort you out something in vice. Not at your previous pay grade, I'm afraid, but you can't have everything. You've got your pension at any rate.

Dave   But you said . . . you said you'd take care of me. I've done everything you've asked for. I've broken myself into fucking pieces to deliver what you wanted.

Jimmy   Yes. And we appreciate that. It's what the pension's there for.

He turns to go.

Dave   This is all I know. All I've ever done. You can't leave me like this.

Jimmy   What do you want me to do? Hold your fucking hand? Think I've done enough of that, don't you? You're out. That's it. End of.

Jimmy *turns to go.*

Dave   What if I stay? You can't force me to leave.

Jimmy   Why the fuck would you say something so stupid?

Dave   What have I got to come back to? Leanne's gone. The kids . . . my life's fucked! All that bullshit about being a legend. Now you're finished with me, you don't give a fuck.

Jimmy   A legend? Don't make me laugh. You're not James fucking Bond. You're a foot soldier. A grunt. The Unit made it all happen for you. Gave you everything you needed. Told you what to say and what to do. Covered your mistakes without you even knowing we were there. You've been a deep swimmer, no doubt about it, but if you turn on us now, we'll hold you under until you're floating face down. Don't think we won't.

Jimmy *puts on his jacket and goes, leaving* **Dave** *in despair.*

Scene Twenty-Two

May 2009.

Dave *is sitting on a chair staring into space.* **Mel** *brings in a cup of tea and a slice of toast or something.*

Mel   Why don't you eat something?

Dave *doesn't reply.*

Mel   It might make you feel better if you do. You haven't eaten for two days.

She moves towards him but **Dave** *turns his chair away.*

Mel   Do you think you should see a doctor? It's not right to spend all day staring at the wall.

Dave   There was a car there.

Mel   Where?

Dave   Outside. Today and yesterday. Two men in a car.

Mel   I didn't see that.

Dave   The Mondeo. The blue Mondeo. Right outside. Not even hiding round the corner but full in front of the house.

Mel   I didn't see anyone in a blue car.

Dave   Because you're not looking properly. Look!

He points at the window. She looks.

Mel   It's just an empty car.

Dave   There were men in it earlier. Just sitting there. Watching. Watching and talking and watching.

Mel   Why would anyone be watching us?

Dave   They're on to me.

Mel   Who? Who's on to you? Look, why don't we go out? Go for a walk or . . .

Dave   I can't leave the house. They'll follow me.

Mel   No one's out there.

Dave   Yes they are! They are. They fucking are!

Mel *goes over to the window and looks out.*

Mel   There's no one there.

Dave   THERE IS!

He grabs her arm too tight. **Mel** *pulls away.*

Mel   You're scaring me.

Dave   Why won't you believe me?

Mel   Because I don't see anyone out there.

Dave   I need to get away. Somewhere they can't find me. Somewhere no one can find me.

Mel   Look, let's go for a walk and then we can see if anyone is following us, okay? We can walk into town and come back and if we see that car or those men you think you saw –

Dave   I did see them –

Mel   If we see them, if we both see them, then we'll know. (*Beat.*) You've not been sleeping. You don't know what tricks your mind is playing. Isn't it better to find out?

Beat.

Dave   Okay. Okay. We'll walk.

Mel *puts her coat on, then turns to* **Dave**.

Mel   Come on then. There might not be anyone there.

Dave   They know that I was involved.

Mel   In Ratcliffe? They know everyone involved. They arrested all of you. Everyone's waiting to go to trial.

Dave   You don't understand. What if they start looking into my past? This could all be a front. Just waiting to catch me on my own and then . . .

Mel   You've got a lawyer. Everyone's hopeful. I promise you, no one's after you.

Dave *suddenly goes and puts his arms around her and starts to cry.*

Dave   I'm sorry. I'm sorry. I'm so sorry. I've let you down. I've let everyone down.

Mel   You haven't.

Dave   I have. I've fucked it all up. I tried my best. I really did but it's not good enough. Nothing's ever good enough.

Mel   Dave, please. You're not making any sense. No one thinks you've fucked up. Least of all me. (*Beat.*) It's going to be okay. I promise. Trust me. Please trust me. Will you trust me?

She gently disengages from him, then holds out her hand.

Come on.

He finally takes it and they leave on their walk.

Scene Twenty-Three

July 2009.

Mel *and* **Gavin** *sit opposite each other, a phone on the table between them.*

Mel   Did she say what time she'd call?

Gavin   No.

Mel   But she did say this morning?

Gavin   Yes.

Mel   But not what time?

Gavin   She said she'd call as soon as she had the papers.

Mel   But it was definitely today?

Gavin   Mel. Asking me the same questions over and over isn't going to make it happen any faster.

Mel   Sorry. Sorry. I feel so . . . crazy. I can't believe he would vanish like this. Just leave a note. No address. Phone's dead. Why would he do this? I don't even know what I'm saying. (*Beat.*) I keep thinking I'm dreaming and I'm going to wake up and this will all be . . . but it's not, is it? It's real.

Gavin   Do you want some tea?

Mel   Haven't you got anything stronger? To take the edge off?

Gavin *gets out a hip flask and waves it at her.*

Mel   You're an angel.

Gavin   An angel and a hairy Scotsman. (*Realises what he's said.*) Sorry.

Mel   Do you remember that day?

Gavin   I do indeed.

Mel   He was trying so hard to make you like him and you . . .

Gavin   I was jealous.

Mel   I know. Won you over though, didn't he?

Gavin   Aye, he did. Won us both over.

Beat.

Mel   And there was nothing under David Cross?

Gavin   No. Not on his birth date. Only David Burton.

Mel   But the passport he travelled with, the one that he used, that said 'David Cross'.

Gavin   I know, but when we looked . . . there was nothing there.

Mel   Maybe it's something from when he was a courier?
Maybe he invented Dave Cross to get away from that life?
Like he said but the other way around.

Gavin   Maybe.

Mel   But if that was true then why not tell me? There was
nothing we couldn't say to each other. Why disappear without
a word?

Gavin   I don't know.

Beat.

Mel   What if there's someone else?

Gavin   No.

Mel   Another woman –

Gavin   No. No way. You'd have known.

Mel   A wife even, hidden away. You hear about cases like
that, don't you? Men with two women, two lives.

Gavin   But he was here all the time. When would he have
had time to be with anyone else?

Mel   When he was working away sometimes I couldn't get
hold of him. He'd always say that his phone had died or he
hadn't heard it or whatever. I never thought anything of it
because he was always so straight up about everything. I
know it's completely crazy and I can't believe I'm saying this
but right now . . . right now if I had to choose . . . if I had to
choose . . . I'd rather he was with another woman than . . .
than . . .

Gavin   He's not dead. Don't even think that.

Mel   Then where is he?!

Gavin   I don't know, but if he was dead, we'd have heard
something. There'd be a . . . a . . . body. We need to stay with
what we know. And all that we know is that he had a passport
in another name and there's no birth certificate for David

Cross. That's it. There could be any number of reasons for that.

Mel   There are, aren't there? Any number of reasons.

Beat.

Gavin   Why did you never tell me about the passport?

Mel   He was so upset when I found it. Devastated. Like he hated himself for letting me down. He looked . . . ashamed. Did I do the wrong thing?

Gavin   No. No. I'd have done the same. He's our friend. We love him. Why wouldn't we believe him?

Mel   I can't believe he'd leave me like this. He wasn't unkind or thoughtless or cruel . . . he was a good man. He cared about everyone. Took time with everyone, didn't he?

Gavin   He did. Everyone loves Dave. There's not a person who has a bad word to say about him.

Beat.

Mel   He used to do things all the time to make me feel special. One time he told me he had a surprise for me. We got in the van and drove right out into the countryside. I kept asking where we were going but he wouldn't say. He pulled over in the middle of nowhere and we got out of the van and he started walking up this hill. I said I wouldn't go on unless he told me what was happening but he just smiled and told me to keep going. That I'd like it when I saw it. We got to the top and he'd made this huge land sculpture out of twigs and rocks. It must have taken hours and it said 'I love you'. Right across the hillside. (*Beat.*) Every morning I wake up and for a moment, I don't know and then . . . it comes rushing in and this . . . balloon of anxiety inflates in my chest until I can hardly breathe and I realise that I might never see him again. (*Breaks down.*) Oh God!

Gavin *goes and puts his arm around her.*

Gavin   We'll find him. Angie's checking for us. We'll find him.

Mel   Was it my fault? Did I push him away? Did I do something . . . anything –

Gavin   Dave loves you. I never saw anything like the two of you. I'd catch him watching you and the look on his face . . . You were everything to him. Whatever's happened, whatever we find out, that's what I saw.

Mel   No matter which way I go, something terrible has happened that can't be undone.

The phone rings. They both look at it.

You answer it. I can't . . . I can't do it.

Gavin *answers the phone.*

Gavin (*to phone*)   Hi. Yes. She's here with me. Right. Okay. What?

He turns away to finish the call. **Mel** *is on tenterhooks.* **Gavin** *ends the call and looks back at* **Mel***.*

Mel   What? What's happened? You've got to tell me, Gav. Whatever it is.

Gavin   He's . . .

Beat.

Mel   Tell me.

Gavin   Dave's a police officer.

Mel   What? No. I don't believe it.

Gavin   Mel . . . She knows what she's talking about.

Mel   No. No. I won't believe it. Tell me this isn't true. Tell me this isn't happening!

But **Gavin** *has no words.*

Loud, clashing, terrifying music overwhelms everything, playing out **Mel***'s state of mind until blackout.*

Scene Twenty-Four

September 2009. **Mel** *is sitting in the dark on the sofa.* **Gavin** *comes in with* **Emma** *and turns the lights on.* **Mel** *hardly moves.*

Gavin   Mel?

She doesn't move.

Melly. I've brought Emma to see you.

He beckons **Emma** *in.* **Mel** *looks at her and then looks away.*

Mel   I told you. I don't want to talk to anyone.

Emma *steps forward.*

Emma   Mel?

Mel   Leave me alone. Please.

Gavin   Ach, don't be like . . .

Mel   I don't want to see anyone. I can't . . . Gav, please. Tell her to go.

Gavin *turns to* **Emma***.*

Gavin   I'm sorry, Emma. I shouldn't have brought you without making sure –

But **Emma** *is past him and sits next to* **Mel***.*

Emma   Please, Mel. Give me five minutes. Just five minutes. Then if you want me to, I'll go.

Beat. **Mel** *nods.*

Emma   I fell in love with a man years ago. The perfect man. Everything I wanted him to be . . . he was. We were so in love. When we were together, I let him guide me towards certain campaigns, certain people who, because of my history with them, let him in. He was part of our group, part of our lives. And then one day he was gone.

Mel   I'm sorry but that isn't what happened to me. I didn't just . . . meet someone who left me –

Emma   He didn't leave. He vanished. Completely.

Now she has **Mel**'*s attention.*

Emma   Left a note to say that he couldn't carry on with life the way it was. It was like a suicide note. I couldn't sleep for thinking of him, somewhere alone and afraid or in pain. I had to find him. But everywhere I looked was a dead end. Finally, I went to the place where he told me he'd grown up, where his parents lived, but there was no trace of him. The man I loved didn't exist. He was a figment, a creation, sent to spy on me and my friends. To infiltrate our lives, win our trust and then betray us.

Mel   We shared . . . everything. Every moment, every thought . . . I told him things . . . things I could hardly dare admit to myself. Things I'd never want anyone else to know. And every single thing . . . someone was listening . . . watching us. Telling him what to do. He used to put his head in my lap and sob about how I was the only family he had –

Emma   About how you were the only person in the world he'd ever loved –

Mel   How special I was –

Emma   – how everything you believed was everything he believed. (*Beat.*) I wanted kids. I really did. Always thought I'd have them. But I've never been able to let anyone get close enough to have another relationship let alone make that step. I was too scared, too wary and now . . . now it's too late. That choice . . . it was stolen from me.

Mel   They've won.

Emma   No, they haven't. Because you've linked man and cover. We've never had that before so it was impossible to move forward. Now we can make them accountable for what they've done. Force them into the light. There are more women.

Mel   How many more?

Emma   Ten . . . so far. But dozens, possibly, over thirty years.

Mel   What's the point? If this shows anything it's that it's only a democracy if you toe the line. You want to voice any other opinions you get spied on, lied to, your life turned upside down.

Emma   But they've made a huge mistake because they thought we didn't matter. To them we were just stupid women who would get rejected and crumble away. Or sluts who didn't care who they slept with. They thought they could do anything they liked to us and get away with it. But they can't.

Mel   Can't they?

Emma   You tell me.

Scene Twenty-Five

Valentine's Day. 2011.

A pub. **Dave** *is waiting at a table.* **Mel** *comes in and he gets to his feet. She hesitates then walks to him. He almost might hug or kiss her but her body language says no way.*

Dave   Can you believe this? Fucking Valentine's Day. I've been so off the wall, I didn't think when I said . . . (*Beat.*) I didn't think you'd come.

Mel   I didn't think I would either but . . .

Dave   Sorry it's taken me so long to get in touch. I wasn't . . . well for quite a while. Couldn't get out of bed. Not like me. I've always been one for getting up early but –

Mel   What do you want, Dave?

Dave   To see you.

Mel   You've had over a year to see me.

Dave   I wasn't well, like I said and once I felt a bit . . . I was . . . Fuck, I'm nervous which seems so fucking . . . Never thought I'd be nervous of you.

Mel   I don't even know who you are.

Dave   Yes you do. I'm Dave Cross.

Mel   No you're not. You're David Burton and I don't know him at all. I know what he looks like and sounds like and I could identify him in the dark from a hundred miles away but . . . everything I thought I knew about that person is a lie.

Dave   Dave Cross never lied to you.

Mel   Is your father dead? (*Beat.*) Is your father dead?

Dave   No.

Mel   I opened my heart to you at the worst moment of my life and you've turned that entire memory into a lie.

Dave   Not a lie. I never lied. I just . . . I wanted you to be okay.

Mel   You know, when you first disappeared I thought it was because of me. Blamed myself.

Dave   It was a difficult time. I couldn't think straight. There was so much pressure on me from all sides. There wasn't room in my head –

Mel   You should have made room! I can understand that to the people in charge, the people telling you what to do, I was just some faceless woman to be used and thrown away, a tool of the trade. But I wasn't to you. I was real. Flesh and blood. And you carried on anyway.

Dave   I'm sorry.

Mel   Sorry doesn't change anything. (*Beat.*) Do you know what I can't stop thinking? Who would I have become over the last six years if I hadn't met you? What paths could my life have taken if you hadn't been there? All my choices were based on us when there was no 'us'. No words can alter that. You made so much sense to me, but you've turned my life upside down and now nothing makes sense . . . nothing at all.

Dave   I wanted to tell you. I nearly did so many times but we were so happy and in love and –

Mel   Love! Do you know what I think? I think you loved having two lives. Being two different people. Good cop and bad cop. You got to have it all.

Dave   It wasn't like that.

Mel   Then what was it like? Tell me something true. Not some bullshit you think I want to hear. Was any of it real?

Dave   Yes. Yes. There were days when even I didn't know what was real and what was cover or who I really was. But what I felt for you was the one thing I held on to. I never wanted to lose who I was through your eyes. I wanted that version of myself to live for ever.

Mel   Do you know what I'm having to do as part of the case? In order for them to realise what they've done to me, what you've done to me, I've had to focus on all my failures at life. So they can put a price on it and pay me off. You've made me become nothing but failure. That's my version of myself.

Dave   You're not a failure.

Mel   Yes, I am. You made me feel so special and now . . . now I just feel stupid. For all those years when I thought I was building something, I've got dust and ashes. And do you know what the worst thing is? The worst thing . . . the worst thing . . . I still fucking love you. I still have . . . all these feelings and it's agony and they're going to be there in some way for the rest of my life. Like this huge scar across my heart. And I don't know if it will ever fade. I always thought that I'd have children, that we'd have children but now . . . I don't know if I can ever trust anyone again. If love will ever be possible for me . . . if I will ever have the chance . . . (*She's overwhelmed.*) I should never have come here. I should never have seen you.

Dave *reaches out to her but* **Mel***'s on her feet moving away from him.*

Dave   Mel –

Mel   Don't touch me. Please don't touch me.

Dave *is on his feet now too.*

Dave   Why can't we make it work from here? You and me. I'll do anything to make things right. To prove I'm who you thought I was.

Long long pause. They gaze at each other. Then **Mel** *shakes her head.*

Mel   I can't.

Dave   Don't say that.

Mel   I can't just forget what you've done.

Dave   You can.

Mel   No. There is no fairytale ending to this story. You might have lived your life like an exciting double agent in a film but you don't get the girl.

She turns to go.

Dave   What if I helped you?

She turns back.

Gave your lawyers all the information they needed. Who approved what and who knew what. What if I did that? Would you forgive me?

Mel   How could I believe a word of it? How could anyone?

Dave   I've got proof. Reports. Signatures. I can draw you the whole chain of command from me to the head of the Unit

to the Home Office to Downing Street. I'd give you it all,
I would. Would we have a chance then?

Long pause.

Mel   There's a hearing next month. If you're there, if you
speak on our side then I might think that you can maybe tell
the truth.

Dave   I'll be there. I'll come and tell them everything they
need to know about the Unit.

Mel   Then I'll see you there.

She walks away and he calls after her.

Dave   Mel!

She turns.

We're going to be so happy.

Scene Twenty-Six

March 2011.

The ante-room at the hearing. **Bev** *and* **Mel** *are there.* **Emma** *comes in.*

Emma   They're calling you.

Mel   I can't do it.

Emma   Yes, you can.

Mel   You've seen what they're doing in there. They're
smearing us in any way they can. They don't care about the
truth or changing anything. They just want to discredit us.
Bury us under a load of insinuation and then shut us up by
paying us off. I can't bear to bleed out my pain and it not
mean anything.

Bev   It will mean something.

Beat.

Mel   He didn't come.

Emma   Are you surprised?

Mel   I wanted some part of him to be the person I loved because then all those years might have been real in some way. But this proves it was nothing but lies.

Emma   Even if bits were real, it's not right, what they've done . . . We have to fight this, stop it happening to anyone else. Stand up and tell the truth. Because otherwise they can pretend it never happened and carry on. Now we've started to speak, people will listen and if they don't, we keep talking until they hear us.

Mel   But I don't believe in this process. I don't believe in anything any more. I was so certain about myself. Then I fell in love with someone who stood for everything I hated. So how can I be sure of anything now?

Bev   You can be sure of us. Because we've all suffered the same. But we can change things. Isn't that what got us here? What made us targets to start with? That we believed we had the power to make things different. Let's be what they feared. Let's be their worst nightmare. They can't silence us all.

Emma *and* **Bev** *come and stand beside her. She looks at them.*

Mel   Do you really believe that? That we can we stop this? Make sure it never happens again?

Bev   Yes.

Emma   But we must all do it together. (*Beat.*) Are you ready?

Beat.

Mel   Yes, yes I am.

Bev *and* **Emma** *leave.* **Cara** *appears on the other side of the stage. She and* **Mel** *look at each other, then face the audience ready for* **Mel** *to give her evidence.*

The End

DRAMA ONLINE

A new way to study drama

From curriculum classics
to contemporary writing
Accompanied by
theory and practice

Discover. Read. Study. Perform.

Find out more:
www.dramaonlinelibrary.com

BLOOMSBURY

methuen
drama

THE ARDEN
SHAKESPEARE

FABER
DIGITAL

Bloomsbury Methuen Drama Modern Plays

include work by

Bola Agbaje
Edward Albee
Davey Anderson
Jean Anouilh
John Arden
Peter Barnes
Sebastian Barry
Alistair Beaton
Brendan Behan
Edward Bond
William Boyd
Bertolt Brecht
Howard Brenton
Amelia Bullmore
Anthony Burgess
Leo Butler
Jim Cartwright
Lolita Chakrabarti
Caryl Churchill
Lucinda Coxon
Curious Directive
Nick Darke
Shelagh Delaney
Ishy Din
Claire Dowie
David Edgar
David Eldridge
Dario Fo
Michael Frayn
John Godber
Paul Godfrey
James Graham
David Greig
John Guare
Mark Haddon
Peter Handke
David Harrower
Jonathan Harvey
Iain Heggie

Robert Holman
Caroline Horton
Terry Johnson
Sarah Kane
Barrie Keeffe
Doug Lucie
Anders Lustgarten
David Mamet
Patrick Marber
Martin McDonagh
Arthur Miller
D. C. Moore
Tom Murphy
Phyllis Nagy
Anthony Neilson
Peter Nichols
Joe Orton
Joe Penhall
Luigi Pirandello
Stephen Poliakoff
Lucy Prebble
Peter Quilter
Mark Ravenhill
Philip Ridley
Willy Russell
Jean-Paul Sartre
Sam Shepard
Martin Sherman
Wole Soyinka
Simon Stephens
Peter Straughan
Kate Tempest
Theatre Workshop
Judy Upton
Timberlake Wertenbaker
Roy Williams
Snoo Wilson
Frances Ya-Chu Cowhig
Benjamin Zephaniah

Bloomsbury Methuen Drama Contemporary Dramatists
include

John Arden (two volumes)
Arden & D'Arcy
Peter Barnes (three volumes)
Sebastian Barry
Mike Bartlett
Dermot Bolger
Edward Bond (eight volumes)
Howard Brenton (two volumes)
Leo Butler
Richard Cameron
Jim Cartwright
Caryl Churchill (two volumes)
Complicite
Sarah Daniels (two volumes)
Nick Darke
David Edgar (three volumes)
David Eldridge (two volumes)
Ben Elton
Per Olov Enquist
Dario Fo (two volumes)
Michael Frayn (four volumes)
John Godber (four volumes)
Paul Godfrey
James Graham
David Greig
John Guare
Lee Hall (two volumes)
Katori Hall
Peter Handke
Jonathan Harvey (two volumes)
Iain Heggie
Israel Horovitz
Declan Hughes
Terry Johnson (three volumes)
Sarah Kane
Barrie Keeffe
Bernard-Marie Koltès (two volumes)
Franz Xaver Kroetz
Kwame Kwei-Armah
David Lan
Bryony Lavery
Deborah Levy
Doug Lucie

David Mamet (four volumes)
Patrick Marber
Martin McDonagh
Duncan McLean
David Mercer (two volumes)
Anthony Minghella (two volumes)
Tom Murphy (six volumes)
Phyllis Nagy
Anthony Neilson (two volumes)
Peter Nichol (two volumes)
Philip Osment
Gary Owen
Louise Page
Stewart Parker (two volumes)
Joe Penhall (two volumes)
Stephen Poliakoff (three volumes)
David Rabe (two volumes)
Mark Ravenhill (three volumes)
Christina Reid
Philip Ridley (two volumes)
Willy Russell
Eric-Emmanuel Schmitt
Ntozake Shange
Sam Shepard (two volumes)
Martin Sherman (two volumes)
Christopher Shinn
Joshua Sobel
Wole Soyinka (two volumes)
Simon Stephens (three volumes)
Shelagh Stephenson
David Storey (three volumes)
C. P. Taylor
Sue Townsend
Judy Upton
Michel Vinaver (two volumes)
Arnold Wesker (two volumes)
Peter Whelan
Michael Wilcox
Roy Williams (four volumes)
David Williamson
Snoo Wilson (two volumes)
David Wood (two volumes)
Victoria Wood

For a complete listing of Bloomsbury
Methuen Drama titles, visit:

www.bloomsbury.com/drama

Follow us on Twitter and keep up to date
with our news and publications

@MethuenDrama